MADNESS, RACK, AND HONEY

MADNESS, RACK,
AND HONEY

COLLECTED LECTURES

MARY RUEFLE

WAVE BOOKS

SEATTLE AND

NEW YORK

Published by Wave Books

www.wavepoetry.com

Wave Books titles are distributed to the trade by

Consortium Book Sales and Distribution

Phone: 800-283-3572 / SAN 631-760X

This title is available in limited edition hardcover

directly from the publisher

Owing to limitations of space, permissions

acknowledgments appear on pages 325–26.

Library of Congress Cataloging-in-Publication Data

Ruefle, Mary, 1952–

Madness, rack, and honey : collected lectures /

Mary Ruefle.—1st ed.

p. cm.

Includes bibliographical references.

ISBN 978-1-933517-57-5 (alk. paper)

1. Poetry—History and criticism. 2. Poetry—

Authorship. 3. Poetics. I. Title.

PN1136.R74 2012

809.1—dc23

2011049617

Designed and composed by Quemadura

ILLUSTRATIONS: pp. 25–26: from Yeats's *A Vision*;

pp. 158: drawing by the author; pp. 165: collage by the author

Printed in the United States of America

9 8 7 6 5 4 3

INTRODUCTION

I never set out to write this book. In 1994 I began to be required to deliver standing lectures to graduate students, and the requirement terrified me. I was told the students preferred informal spontaneous talks, but I am a rotten and unsteady extemporizer. I preferred to write my lectures because I am a writer and writing is my natural act, more natural than speaking.

I always looked askance at writing on writing, but I'm intelligent enough to see that writing is writing. Still, my allegiance to poetry, to art, is greater than my allegiance to knowledge and intelligence, and that stance is harder and harder to maintain in today's world, because knowledge and intelligence form the corporate umbrella (the academy) that shelters and protects poetry in a culture that cares about other things. On the other hand, the evening news tells us a corporation is not interested in protecting anything other than itself. This is best contemplated by the younger generation, on whom it will have the greatest impact.

I see this book as my having learned, step by step, how to think and talk about poetry in ways and terms that are my own, and when these ways became boring to me, I began to break down my methods; anyone can see the lectures become increasingly fragmentary and turn, who knows, even against themselves.

I do not think I really have anything to say about poetry other than remarking that it is a wandering little drift of unidentified sound, and trying to say more reminds me of following the sound of a thrush into the woods on a summer's eve—if you persist in following the thrush it will only recede deeper and deeper into the woods; you will never actually see the thrush (the hermit thrush is especially shy), but I suppose listening is a kind of knowledge, or as close as one can come. "Fret not after knowledge, I have none," is what the thrush says. Perhaps we can use our knowledge to preserve a bit of space where his lack of knowledge can survive.

MADNESS, RACK, AND HONEY

ON BEGINNINGS

In life, the number of beginnings is exactly equal to the number of endings: no one has yet to begin a life who will not end it.

In poetry, the number of beginnings so far exceeds the number of endings that we cannot even conceive of it. Not every poem is finished—one poem is abandoned, another catches fire and is carried away by the wind, which may be an ending, but it is the ending of a poem without an end.

Paul Valéry, the French poet and thinker, once said that no poem is ever ended, that every poem is merely abandoned. This saying is also attributed to Stéphane Mallarmé, for where quotations begin is in a cloud.

Paul Valéry also described his perception of first lines so vividly, and to my mind so accurately, that I have never forgotten it: the opening line of a poem, he said, is like finding a fruit on the ground, a piece of fallen fruit you have never seen before, and the poet's task is to create the tree from which such a fruit would fall.

In the beginning was the Word. Western civilization rests upon those words. And yet there is a lively group of thinkers who believe that in the beginning was the Act. That nothing can precede action—no breath before act, no thought before act, no pervasive love before some kind of act.

I believe the poem is an act of the mind. I think it is easier to talk about the end of a poem than it is to talk about its beginning. Because the poem ends on the page, but it begins off the page, it begins in the mind. The mind acts, the mind wills a poem, often against our own will; somehow this happens, somehow a poem gets written in the middle of a chaotic holiday party that has just run out of ice, and it's your house.

An act of the mind. To move, to make happen, to make manifest. By an act of Congress. A state of real existence rather than possibility. And poets love possibility! They love to wonder and explore. Hard lot! But the poem, no matter how full of possibility, has to *exist*! To conduct oneself, to behave. How a poem acts marks its individual character. A poem by Glandolyn Blue does not sound like a poem by Timothy Sure. To pretend, feign, impersonate. That, too, yes and always, because self-consciousness is its own pretension, and has been from its beginning; the human mind is capable of a great elastic theater. As the poet Ralph Angel puts it, "The poem is an interpretation of weird theatrical shit." The weird theatrical shit is what goes on around us every day of our lives; an animal of only instinct, Johnny Ferret, has in his actions drama, but no theater; theater requires that you draw a circle around the action and observe it from outside the circle; in other words, self-consciousness *is* theater.

Everyone knows that if you query poets about how their poems begin, the answer is always the same: a phrase, a line, a scrap of language, a rhythm, an image, something seen, heard, witnessed, or imagined. And the lesson is always the same, and young poets recognize this to be one of the most important lessons they can learn: if you have any idea for a poem, an exact grid of intent, you are on the wrong path, a dead-end alley, at the top of a cliff you haven't even climbed. This is a lesson that can only be learned by trial and error.

I believe many fine poems begin with ideas, but if you tell too many faces this, or tell it too loudly, they will get the wrong idea.

Now here is something really interesting (to me), something you can use at a standing-up-only party when everyone is tired of hearing there are one million three thousand two hundred ninety-five words used by the Eskimo for snow. This is what Ezra Pound learned from Ernest Fenollosa: Some languages are so constructed—English among them—that we each only really speak one sentence in our lifetime. That sentence begins with your first words, toddling around the kitchen, and ends with your last words right before you step into the limousine, or in a nursing home, the night-duty attendant vaguely on hand. Or, if you are blessed, they are heard by someone who knows you and loves you and will be sorry to hear the sentence end.

When I told Mr. Angel about the lifelong sentence, he said: "That's a lot of semicolons!" He is absolutely right; the sentence would be unwieldy and awkward and resemble the novel of a savant, but the next time you use a semicolon (which, by the way, is the least-used mark of punctuation in all of poetry) you should stop and be thankful that there exists this little thing, invented by a human being—an Italian as a matter of fact—that allows us to go on and keep on connecting speech that for all apparent purposes is unrelated.

You might say a poem *is* a semicolon, a living semicolon, what connects the first line to the last, the act of keeping together that whose nature is to fly apart. Between the first and last lines there exists—a poem—and if it were not for the poem that intervenes, the first and last lines of a poem would not speak to each other.

Would not speak to each other. Because the lines of a poem are speaking to each other, not you to them or they to you.

I will tell you what I miss: I miss watching a movie and at the end, huge scrolled words come on the screen and say: The End. I miss finishing a novel and there on the last page, at a discrete distance from the last words of the last sentence, are the dark letters spelling The End.

It was its own thrill. I didn't ignore them, I read them, even if only silently, with a deep sense of feeling: both the feeling of being replete, a feeling of satisfaction, and the feeling of loss, the sadness of having finished the book.

I have never, in my life, read a poem that ended with the words *The End*. Why is that, I wonder. I think perhaps the brevity of poems compared to novels makes one feel that there has been no great sustention of energy, no marathon worthy of pulling tape across the finish line. And then I found a poem of mine that I had carefully written by hand in the sixth grade, and at the bottom of the page, in India ink, beautifully apart from the rest of the text, were the words *The End*. And I realized children very often denote the end because it is indeed a great achievement for them to have written anything, and they are completely unaware of the number of stories and poems that have already been written; they know *some*, of course, but have not yet found out the extent to which they are not the only persons residing on the planet. And so they sign their poems and stories like kings. Which is a wonderful thing.

Roland Barthes suggests there are three ways to finish any piece of writing: the ending will have the last word or the ending will be silent or the ending will execute a pirouette, do something unexpectedly incongruent.

Gaston Bachelard says the single most succinct and astonishing thing: We begin in admiration and we end by organizing our disappointment. The moment of admiration is the experience of something unfiltered, vital and fresh—it could also be horror—and the moment of organization is both the onset of disappointment and its dignification; the least we can do is dignify our knowingness, the loss of some vitality through familiarization, by admiring not the thing itself but how we can organize it, think about it.

I am afraid there is no way around this. It is the one true inevitable thing. And if you believe that, then you are conceding that in the beginning was the act, not the word.

The painter Cy Twombly quotes John Crowe Ransom, on a scrap of paper: "The image cannot be dispossessed of a primordial freshness which ideas can never claim."

Easy and appropriate thing for a painter to say. Cy Twombly uses text in some of his drawings and paintings, usually poetry, usually Dante. Many men and women have written long essays and lectures on the ideas they see expressed in Twombly's work.

Bachelard's sentence simply says this: origins (beginnings) have consequences (endings).

The poem is the consequence of its origins. Give me the fruit and I will take from it a seed and plant it and watch grow the tree from which it fell.

Barbara Herrnstein Smith, in her book *Poetic Closure: A Study of How Poems End*, says this: "Perhaps all we can say, and even this may be too much, is that varying degrees or states of tension seem to be involved in all our experiences, and that the most gratifying ones are those in which whatever tensions are created are also released. Or, to use another familiar set of terms, an experience is gratifying to the extent that those expectations that are aroused are also fulfilled."

But there is no book I know of on the subject of how poems begin. How can the origin be *traced* when there is no form or shape that precedes it to trace? It is exactly like tracing the moment of the big bang—we can go back to a nanosecond before the beginning, before the universe burst into being, but we can't go back to the precise beginning because that would precede knowledge, and we can't "know" anything before "knowing" itself was born.

I have flipped through books, reading hundreds of opening and closing lines, across ages, across cultures, across aesthetic schools, and I have discovered that first lines are remarkably similar, even repeated, and that last lines are remarkably similar, even repeated. Of course in all cases they remain remarkably distinct, because the words belong to completely different poems. And I began to realize, reading these first and last lines, that there are not only the first and last lines of the lifelong sentence we each speak but also the first and last lines of the long piece of language delivered to us by others, by those we listen to. And in the best of all possible lives, that beginning and that end are the same: in poem after poem I encountered words that mark the first something made out of language that we hear as children repeated night after night, like a refrain: *I love you. I am here with you. Don't be afraid. Go to sleep now.* And I encountered words that mark the last something made out of language that we hope to hear on earth: *I love you. You are not alone. Don't be afraid. Go to sleep now.*

But it is growing damp and I must go in. Memory's fog is rising. Among Emily Dickinson's last words (in a letter). A woman whom everyone thought of as shut-in, homebound, cloistered, spoke as if she had been *out*, exploring the earth, her whole life, and it was finally time to go in. And it was.

9

POETRY AND THE MOON

LOOK DOWN FAIR MOON.

Look down fair moon and bathe this scene,
Pour softly down night's nimbus floods on faces ghastly,
   swollen, purple,
On the dead on their backs with arms toss'd wide,
Pour down your unstinted nimbus sacred moon.

1865

RECONCILIATION.

Word over all, beautiful as the sky,
Beautiful that war and all its deeds of carnage must in
   time be utterly lost,
That the hands of the sisters Death and Night incessantly
   softly wash again, and ever again, this soil'd world;
For my enemy is dead, a man divine as myself is dead,

I look where he lies white-faced and still in the coffin—I
　draw near,
Bend down and touch lightly with my lips the white face in
　the coffin.

1865–66

If you read through the collected shorter poems of Whitman—
especially those brief lyrics in, say, *Drum-Taps* or *Sands at Sev-*
enty—you'll notice that often Whitman will follow a poem in
which he is not present with a poem on the same subject in
which he *is* present. Call it a compulsion, it's a delightful pat-
tern as he rewrites his every impulse with himself at the center.
The second poem I have given you here, "Reconciliation," is a
famous poem, but I like the first, not so famous, and clearly a
lunar paraphrase of the second. Of course it was written first,
and that makes the second a human paraphrase of the first. The
faces in the first poem are purple, swollen, ghastly; the scene is
obviously a battlefield, none of the corpses have been washed
and put in a coffin as they are about to be in "Reconciliation."
And only then, after the moon has bathed them, does it occur
to Whitman to kiss them. In fact, I think the moon is every-
where present in the second poem, though it is never men-
tioned. It's there in the opening, "Word over all," which of
course refers to the title, "Reconciliation," but is also mindful

of "in the beginning was the Word," which clearly, in the instance of these two poems, can be rendered, "First there was the moon." And it's present in the still, white face of the corpse itself, which Whitman kisses, and as he does so *becomes the moon*. I like to think of the second as a revision of the first, seen by the light of the moon, which has made the kiss, and the poem, possible. The moon *making a poem possible* ... what can we say about that? What *on earth* can we say about poetry and the moon?

I am convinced that the first lyric poem was written at night, and that the moon was witness to the event and that the event was witness to the moon. For me, the moon has always been the very embodiment of lyric poetry. In the West, lyric poetry begins with a woman on an island in the seventh or sixth century BC, and I say now: lyric poetry begins with a woman on an island on a moonlit night, when the moon is nearing full or just the other side of it, or on the dot. Epic poetry was well established. The great men had sung of battles and heroes, whose actions affected thousands, and blinding shields and the wine-dark sea and the rosy-fingered dawn. Yet it is wrong to think that the clamor had died down. Historians tell us the times were not idyllic; in the Aeolian Islands, especially at Lesbos, the civilization was old but rapidly changing, torn by economic

unrest and clashes between emerging political ideas and tradi-
tional principles. In the middle of all this then, a woman on an
island on a moonlit night picks up some kind of writing instru-
ment, or she doesn't, she picks up a musical instrument, or she
doesn't, she begins to simply speak or sing, and the words ex-
press her personal feelings of the moment. Let's call her Sap-
pho. One can hardly say these little songs have survived—for
we have only fragments—but even this seems fitting, for what is
the moment but a fragment of greater time?

TONIGHT I'VE WATCHED

> The moon and then
> the Pleiades
> go down
>
> The night is now
> half-gone; youth
> goes; I am
>
> in bed alone

There is a pervasive sorrow in the poem and not much strug-
gle to change the order of things. The moon *sets*, the night
passes, life *flies*, and the individual is the obvious repository of
all this motion, insofar as she is *aware* of it, is conscious at all,
and yet, *lying alone in her bed* she brings it at once to a stand-

1 3

still; the nauseous motion of the whole system is pinned and preserved like a butterfly upon a board, so that time hardly seems to be passing at all, though that is exactly what the poem is about. It has been noted many times that there are more sad poems than happy poems in this world, and though I have not fed them all into a computer and read the printout, I would guess that the moon occurs more frequently than the sun as an image in lyric poetry. And I wonder, why? I could start with a dozen reasons: insomnia; the moon's association with death, one of poetry's most common themes (yet the moon is equally associated with fertility); or the fact most of the poems in this world have supposedly been written by heterosexual men, who desire women, and the moon is embodied, in so many languages, as a woman, though that's not universally true— German is one of the notable exceptions. One thing leads to another, one thing cancels another thing out, they are all interconnected, and none of them interest me. After all, it has been proved, using highly sensitive equipment, that even a cup of tea is subject to lunar tides. Let me offer a simple observation. There is a greater contrast between the moon and the night sky than there is between the sun and the daytime sky. And this contrast is more conducive to sorrow, which always separates or isolates itself, than it is to happiness, which always joins or blends. And to stand face-to-face with the sun is preposterous—it would blind you. Every child is taught not to stare at the sun. The sun is the source of life itself, the great creative power.

One cannot confront god without instant annihilation; you can't look directly at Medusa, but you can look at her useless reflection. The moon has no light of its own; our apprehension of it is but a reflection of the sun. And some believe artists reflect the creative powers of some original impulse too great to name. Another thing: the moon is the very image of silence —and, as Charles Simic says, "The highest levels of consciousness are wordless." The great lunacy of most lyric poems is that they attempt to use words to convey what cannot be put into words. On the other hand, stars were the first *text*, the first instance of gabbiness; connecting the stars, making a pattern out of them, was the first *story*, sacred to storytellers. But the moon was the first *poem*, in the lyric sense, an entity complete in itself, recognizable at a glance, one that played upon the emotions so strongly that the context of time and place hardly seemed to matter. "Its power lies precisely in its remaining always on the verge of being 'read,'" says Simic, speaking of photography, and I see the moon as the incunabulum of photography, as the first photograph, the first stilled moment, the first study in contrasts. Me here—you there. Now that's an interesting map—only I've got it all wrong. As Paul Auster points out in his novel *Moon Palace*, it really goes like this—"You there—me here." Land maps, the art of cartography, did not exist, could not exist, until *after* the astronomers flourished: "A man can't know where he is on earth except in relation to the moon or a star. . . . A here exists only in relationship to a there, not the other way around." The *there* must come first. The moon is very clearly the Other—capital *O*, full moon *O*—in relationship to which we stand and exist. Every glance at the moon, in whatever phase, pinpoints our existence on earth. For the sky is the only phenomenon that can be seen from all points on the planet. All cultures, without exception, have an experience of the moon. If Ezra Pound claimed that all ages are contemporaneous, Simic says it is because all present moments certainly are. When I lived in China, the people I met were surprised that I made as much of the moon as they did. Apparently they believed the West did not sufficiently appreciate its qualities. Indeed, they have a whole holiday—the mid-autumn festival—given over to the moon. On the night of the full moon in September, families come together after dark and have an outdoor picnic, lit by those round lanterns that are in imitation of the moon, and they eat round food, including the round cakes baked for the occasion and known as mooncakes. The spectators stay put, even on a cloudy night, until the moon can be viewed, however briefly. The Chinese look at the moon and think of some family member or loved one who is not present, and know that on this same evening the absent one is reflecting on them. I myself sat in a circle of unmarried girls who passed the time *imagining* their unknown future husbands looking at the moon and imagining *them*. The lunar image became a form of communication, as indeed all imagery does in poetry: "The eye has knowledge the mind cannot share," says Hayden Carruth.

Neruda, in his poem "Nocturnal Establishments," calls himself a "surviving worshiper of the heavens"—which is what many poets are, I think, yet some say there are two things that call this into question: postmodern theory and technology (which are inseparable) and the Apollo Lunar Landing Missions. There's a popular and interesting book just published on cyberspace—*Being Digital* by Nicholas Negroponte. Without dwelling too much on it—for my heart is really with the Apollo Lunar Landing Missions—I want to comment on a few remarks by Mr. Negroponte. "The digital planet will look and feel like the head of a pin." Comment: with a thousand angels dancing there. Remark: "The slow human handling of most information in the form of books, magazines, newspapers, and videocassettes, is about to become the instantaneous and inexpensive transfer of electronic data that move at the speed of light." Remark, by Keats, on first looking into Chapman's Homer: "Then felt I like some watcher of the skies / When a new planet swims into his ken." I imagine that could occur somewhat near the speed of light, along with all those red wheelbarrows and white chickens standing in the rain. Okay, three seconds—as the approximate duration of the present moment has been defined—not quite the speed of light, but about the time it takes to look at the moon. Really, people must think literary aficionados are all addicted to painfully heavy, slow things. Like the aircraft used for the lunar launches, good books only *look* heavy and slow: their speed depends on their internal engines and where they are pointed. The moon seems like an appropriate link between NASA and poetry. As Julio Cortázar put it: "Man has reached the moon, but twenty centuries ago a poet knew the enchantments that would make the moon come down to earth. Ultimately, what is the difference?" Last fall, a little article called "Poetry and the Moon, 1969" by Edward Lense appeared in the *AWP Chronicle*. Mr. Lense's concerns are not really mine, but to put the article in a nutshell, Mr. Lense effectively uses the moon landing of July 20, 1969, as an exercise in semiotics, showing how in poetry images of the moon changed with the advent of technology. So that we go from the moon of myth—Robert Graves's White Goddess, the muse, the rich gorgeous silvery stuff of Artemis or Diana—to the ambivalent postlanding stuff like Robert Lowell's image of the moon as a dead "chassis orbiting about the earth, / grin of heatwave, spasm of stainless steel, / gadabout with heart of chalk, unnamable / void and cold thing in the universe." The moon at midcentury gets hidden behind smog, gets imprisoned, entombed, finally reduced to ash, as if poets declared, says Mr. Lense, "that metaphoric language could no longer be used for the moon because it had become too prosaic once the astronauts had removed its mystery by landing on it." That seems contradictory to me, since ash, smog, prison, and tombs, when used in relation to the moon, *are* metaphors, and though metaphors change, to say they are abandoned is in error. But I know—you know—what he means. Basically it's like saying a woman is not interesting unless she's a virgin. Lowell was too good a poet to believe this, so his lines actually resonate with some interest, but Mr. Lense also quotes at length and discusses seriously some really dreadful moon-verse written on the occasion of the first moon-landing and published the day after by the *New York Times*—in particular, poems by Babette Deutsch and Anthony Burgess (Mr. Lowell's poem is not included in the *Times*), poems that are so bad I think it is unfair both to the poets themselves, who are not at their best in these occasional verses, and to the general reader, for whom the poems are used as an indicator of how poets responded to the moon landing and its aftereffects on the imagination. Mr. Lense could sensibly argue that a full-page spread of poetry in the *New York Times* is an indicator of something, and he would be right. In fact, the whole of that day's newspaper, which I have read, is rather wonderful. On the front page there is a poem by Archibald MacLeish, a thoroughly mediocre poem that Mr. Lense also discusses and dismisses—it's a vague, positive account and celebration of the moon landing, and includes the earnest, straight-faced line "O, a meaning!" and though MacLeish never says what that meaning is, I think the contrast between how such a line was read in 1969 and how it is read today is an even better indication of the changes that have taken place in poetry. And wasn't it Mr. MacLeish who said, "A poem should not mean, but be"? And, in a remarkable aside that has nothing to do with the moon landing, there is printed on the Letters to the Editor page—without commentary—a poem by Mr. James Kirkup called "Emily in Winter: Amherst." There is extensive coverage of the war in Vietnam and the unrest among students at home; and then there is the page Mr. Lense focuses on, a full-length spread of poems by Babette Deutsch, Anthony Burgess, Anne Sexton, and the Russian Andrei Voznesensky. These are the poets, he says, who level the charge of lunacide against NASA. Lunacide! That's a wonderful word and I thank Mr. Lense for it. But the charge is suicidal. Last summer marked the twenty-fifth anniversary of the moon landing, and I don't think the moon has lost any of her presence. Mr. Lense closes his article with a paragraph beginning: "At the moment, then, the gods in heaven have lost their names, and adequate new names have yet to be invented by poets or anyone else." I wish I had a dollar for every time I have heard that. I am reminded of what Kenzaburo Oe, the Japanese novelist, said recently at a symposium of Nobel Laureates in Atlanta: "It is the second job of literature to create myth. But its first job is to destroy that myth." And, thinking of Mr. Lense's use of the phrase "at the moment" ("At the moment, then, the gods in heaven have lost . . ."), I am reminded of what the great Italian poet of the twentieth century, Eugenio Montale, says in his poem "To Pio Rajna": "He / who digs into the past would know / that barely a millionth of a second / divides the past from the future." I think it is much more interesting—better things get said—to turn from the poetry pages of that old newspaper to the pages of moon-walk response, in the same issue, written in prose by various prominent people of the time. Pablo Picasso: "It means nothing to me. I have no opinion about it, and I don't care." With his moonlike head, alive in his own moment, Picasso struck a pose of isolation, cut off from the pressing issues of the day. What about the astronauts themselves? While they were on the moon, isn't it likely there was at least *one moment* when they were cut off from the pressing matters of the day, their job, the rest of us on Earth—surely!—and fulfilled some private experience of wonder or fear or repose? One notable spoke as if he were an astronaut himself—Vladimir Nabokov: "Treading the soil of the moon, palpitating its pebbles, tasting the panic and splendor of the event, feeling in the pit of one's stomach the separation from terra . . . these form the most romantic sensation an explorer has ever known . . . . this is the only thing I can say about the matter . . . . The utilitarian results do not interest me." The uselessness of poetry rears its head, its basic nonutilitarian nature. But to inhabit the moment is not the exclusive domain of poetry. After all, Neil Armstrong had become a lunatic, literally, *touched by the moon.*

Between 1969 and 1972, six missions left for the moon and six missions came back. Not everyone who reads poetry is changed by the experience, nor were all the men who went to the moon forever altered by their vacation. But those who were, without exception, all say the same thing—it was not being *on* the moon that profoundly affected them as much as it was looking at the *earth* from the vantage point of the moon. The earth became the Other. You there—me here.

Alan Shepard, Apollo 14: "I remember being struck by the fact that it looks so peaceful from that distance, but remembering on the other hand all the confrontation going on all over that planet, and feeling a little sad that people on planet earth couldn't see that same sight because obviously all the military and political differences become so insignificant seeing it from that distance."

Edgar Mitchell, Apollo 14: "For me, it was the beginning of unitary thinking. To think that the molecules of my body were manufactured in the same furnace as those stars in those galaxies billions of years ago." Mitchell left NASA a year after his return and founded the Institute of Noetic Sciences in Northern California, an institution devoted to the study of consciousness, and of how we fit into the universe. In 1994 the institution had 40,000 members. "We went up there as space technicians, and we came back humanitarians. Looking [back] at earth is an instant global consciousness."

James Irwin, Apollo 15: "I felt the power of God as I'd never felt it before." Mr. Irwin, apparently, had an epiphany while on the moon—a year after his mission, he resigned from the Air

Force to found the evangelical High Flight Foundation. He led several expeditions to Turkey's Mt. Ararat in search of evidence of Noah's Ark. He died of a heart attack in 1991, but not before writing this about the moon: "We lived on another world that was completely 'ours' for three days. It must have been very much like the feelings of Adam and Eve when the Earth was 'theirs.' How to describe it, how to describe it."

Alan Bean, Apollo 12: "Every artist has the earth or their imaginations to inspire their paintings. I've got the earth and my imagination, and I'm the first to have the moon too." Mr. Bean is a full-time painter. All he paints are pictures of the moon. "Certainly riding a rocket to the moon is the biggest kick you can have, but when I paint I get the same feeling that I got when I flew in space well. Certainly the view isn't as good, but the best part of life is internal."

Neil Armstrong, Apollo 11: There are no comments by Mr. Armstrong. He lives reclusively in Ohio and does not attend conferences, reunions, celebrations, parades, anniversaries, press events. He does not answer mail from strangers, answer the telephone, open the door. He was however, many years ago, asked how he felt knowing his footprints might remain undisturbed on the lunar surface for centuries. "I hope somebody goes up there some day," he said, "and cleans them up."

One thing is clear from these experiences: the men began with a mission—the Apollo Lunar Landing Mission, one that would affect, technologically, hundreds of thousands of lives through the development of computers, transistors, integrated circuits, and lightweight plastics—and ended with a vision. From mission to vision. Yeats would know exactly what this was all about. According to his ultimate moon-chart, he could have predicted it. When I was in college I read Yeats, and, of course, *A Vision*, that strange supernatural document that was given— spiritually dictated—to Yeats's wife Georgie, beginning in 1917 and ending in 1920, in sessions of automatic writing, in which she became a medium for the unknown and unseen writer—actually a group of them—who later, so as not to fatigue her, came to her while she was asleep and spoke aloud through her while she was sleeping. When I look back at the book now and read some of the passages my nineteen-year-old hand underlined, I sometimes laugh out loud. I don't trust such elaborate and complete systems, I don't trust methods by which we categorize men and humanity, which is exactly what *A Vision* is, a system using the phases of the moon as its metaphor ("We have come to give you metaphors for poetry," the voice said to Yeats), a system that constructs the history of consciousness, both individual and collective, in the past, present, and future. A system that could, say, forecast the birth, or death, of a Christ or a Nietzsche. According to this system, the universe is a great egg that turns itself inside out and then starts building its shell again. So you see, there is still much in *A Vision* that fascinates. I certainly don't have the time here today to devote myself to discussing *A*

TABLE OF THE FOUR FACULTIES

WILL	MASK	CREATIVE MIND	BODY OF FATE
1. No	description except	Complete plasticity.	
2. Beginning of energy.	*True.* Illusion. *False.* Delusion.	*True.* Physical activity. *False.* Cunning.	Enforced love of the world.
3. Beginning of ambition.	*True.* Simplification through intensity. *False.* Dispersal.	*True.* Supersensual receptivity. *False.* Pride.	Enforced love of another.
4. Desire for *primary* objects.	*True.* Intensity through emotions. *False.* Curiosity.	*True.* Beginning of the abstract supersensual. *False.* Fascination of sin.	Enforced intellectual action.
5. Separation from innocence.	*True.* Conviction. *False.* Domination.	*True.* Rhetoric. *False.* Spiritual arrogance.	Enforced belief.
6. Artificial individuality.	*True.* Fatalism. *False.* Superstition.	*True.* Constructive emotion. *False.* Authority.	Enforced emotion.
7. Assertion of individuality.	*True.* Self-analysis. *False.* Self-adaptation.	*True.* Creation through pity. *False.* Self-driven desire.	Enforced sensuality.
8. War between individuality and race.	*True.* Self-immolation. *False.* Self-assurance.	*True.* Amalgamation. *False.* Despair.	The beginning of strength.

WILL	MASK	CREATIVE MIND	BODY OF FATE
9. Belief takes place of individuality.	*True.* Wisdom. *False.* Self-pity.	*True.* Domination of the intellect. *False.* Distortion.	Adventure that excites the individuality.
10. The image-breaker.	*True.* Self-reliance. *False.* Isolation.	*True.* Dramatisation of Mask. *False.* Self-desecration.	Humanity.
11. The consumer. The pyre-builder.	*True.* Consciousness of self. *False.* Self-consciousness.	*True.* Emotional intellect. *False.* The Unfaithful.	Natural law.
12. The Forerunner.	*True.* Self-realization. *False.* Self-abandonment.	*True.* Emotional philosophy. *False.* Enforced lure.	Search.
13. The sensuous man.	*True.* Renunciation. *False.* Emulation.	*True.* Creative imagination through antithetical emotion. *False.* Enforced self-realization.	Interest.
14. The obsessed man.	*True.* Oblivion. *False.* Malignity.	*True.* Vehemence. *False.* Opinionated will.	None except monotony.
15.	No description except	Complete beauty.	

Vision. I want only to speak briefly about two phases of the moon according to the chart.

I want to look briefly at phase one, the new moon, "no description except complete plasticity"; complete plasticity is complete objectivity, pure thought, and the character of the first phase is moral. And at phase fifteen, the full moon, "no description except that this is a phase of complete beauty"; complete beauty is complex subjectivity, pure image; the character of the fifteenth phase is physical. In other words, thought disappears into image and image disappears into thought. Yeats believed that every soul or person was eventually reincarnated into the first and fifteenth phases, which are both pure spirit without a bodily equivalent. Keats, in his lifetime as Keats, was born at phase fourteen, as close as one can come to pure image and still exist, a rather ideal phase for a lyric poet; Yeats calls him an almost perfect type where intellectual curiosity is, though still present, at its weakest, so you have the wonderful cusplike effect of thought and feeling in his work. As Yeats describes it, "The being has almost reached the end of that elaboration of itself which has for its climax an absorption in time." A woman alone at night looking at the moon, and since her character is physical, let's make her naked. But didn't I say earlier that sorrow, the isolated sensuality of so much lyric poetry, seeks to separate itself from its surroundings? How then can it be absorbed into time? It seems that in the moment the final elaboration of oneself is made—when one finally asserts oneself—I am alive and I know it!—the moment expands to its full stature as eternity. Call it gibberish, this is what poetry is famous for. In fact when Yeats says "the being has almost reached the end of that elaboration of itself which has for its climax an absorption in time," he is describing the birth of the lyric poem, that little bit of masturbation, which, if you look at the chart, inevitably had to be preceded by the plasticity, the thoughtful moral character of the great epic poems. But when I look at these charts I think more of Wallace Stevens than I do of Yeats. In Stevens, the sun is used as an image much more often than the moon is. His metaphors are different, but his "poles" are like the new and full moons, and he routinely strips and clothes himself. *Clothe me for I am naked*, says Yeats in most of his poems; *Strip me for I am clothed*, says Stevens in most of his. Indeed, the moon embodies the three principles of poetry as put forth by Stevens in his poem "Notes Toward a Supreme Fiction": (1) *it must be abstract*, as only the pure plasticity of a return to possibility can be abstract, the new moon as an "immaculate beginning," the "original source of the first idea"; (2) *it must change*, the principle by which Nanzia Nunzio, on her trip around the world, loses her virginity; (3) *it must give pleasure*, thus poetry comes round like the moon to its "irrational // Distortion ... the more than rational distortion, / The fiction that results from feeling," and finds in its fullness a final good, though that "final" is part of its fiction.

There are societies on earth today whose inhabitants do not

believe that man has walked on the moon. You might say they believe in a fiction, but that fiction constitutes their way of knowing things. Today I am surprised that, although I was a sentient being living in civilization, I recall very little about the first stroll on the moon, though I know exactly where I was when it happened. But I was not watching it on television and I do not recall what phase the moon was in—that kind of thing. I was in a Belgian taxicab around ten p.m. on that Sunday night in 1969 (had a poet been working at NASA perhaps it would have been scheduled for a Monday), I was on my way to a café— a bar really—where I met my friends for drinks every night of the summer. The driver spoke only Flemish and I only English. He was listening to the radio and suddenly he began to shout and speak rapidly. It took some time for it to register and then I remembered that right about now the Americans were supposed to land on the moon. He pulled over to the side of the road and got out of the cab. I got out too and there was the moon in the night sky—he pointed at it and I nodded and we stood there for a moment, in silence, looking at the moon. Then we got back in the cab and he drove me to the place I wanted most to be, though when I was there I would never admit to any of my friends that I spent the rest of my time alone in my room writing poetry. I even remember an image I was especially fond of in one of those poems—there was some woman wandering around a field carrying a *strawberry wand*! When I paid the driver his fare he pointed again at the moon and said a single word I didn't understand. But one of my friends inside the bar spoke Flemish and later I asked him what it meant. He said it meant *crazy*. But no less an authority than the Dalai Lama tells us the moon to a Buddhist is representative of serenity and repose. Is Sappho's poem, ultimately, one of agitation or repose? I'll let Maurice Blanchot answer that: "Repose in light can be—tends to be—peace through light, light that appeases and gives peace; but repose in light is also repose—deprivation of all external help and impetus—so that nothing comes to disturb, or to pacify, the pure movement of the light. . . . *Repose in light*: is it sweet appeasement through light? Is it the difficult deprivation of oneself and of all of one's own movement, a position in the light without repose? Here two infinitely different experiences are separated by almost nothing." I know it's heavy-handed, but I think this is what happens when we look at the moon, and when we write: in each case, two infinitely different experiences are separated by almost nothing, and that very *nothing* is what is most essential and difficult to maintain. When Buzz Aldrin joined Armstrong on the surface of the moon, his first words were: "Beautiful, beautiful. Magnificent desolation."

ON SENTIMENTALITY

I'd like to begin with a brief commentary on an article that appeared in the March/April 1994 issue of the *AWP Chronicle*. The article is by Philip Sterling and is called "Who We Are: The Pronoun of Intimacy." It is an intelligent and sensitive article against the use of the "vague you" in American poetry—you know, when you read a poem and it employs the pronoun *you* only you are not quite sure who the you is, and the worst possibility is that it just might be a substitute for the pronoun *I*. Perhaps you have encountered this concern in a class. Let's hear Mr. Sterling describe the problem again: "The problem in contemporary poetry . . . is one in which the pronoun does *not* refer to something previously specified . . . nor is it understood on the part of the reader." Mr. Sterling goes on to suggest that authenticity in a poem depends upon a poet's choice of pronoun and that the *vague you* is precisely one of the ills that haunts our verse, though he is not so absurd as to suggest it is the only one. Nonetheless he says it is one of the causes of the "often acknowledged illness" in contemporary poetry. He then prints the first stanza of a poem by Tess Gallagher to show how the poem "contains a confusion or uncertainty of point of view" caused by the *vague you*. I wish I didn't have to read this. I wish I didn't have to argue with it. But, please, *what is the point?* Mr. Sterling asserts we don't *participate* in such poems, but become "a passive observer, an eavesdropper"—as if it were of the utmost importance that we always, always, participate, participate, participate. When was the last time you participated in a poem by Emily Dickinson, no matter what pronoun she was using? Sometimes I feel enormously privileged to be a mere eavesdropper. Mr. Sterling asks a burning question: "After all, how can we know who 'you' is, if 'you' is, in fact, some ill-defined 'I'?" I'd like to answer that: read the poem, use your noggin, and figure it out. If that is difficult for you, then as you read keep in mind what Shelley says in his essay "On Life": "The words *I*, and *you*, and *they*, are grammatical devices invented simply for arrangement and totally devoid of the intense and exclusive sense usually attributed to them." Please don't misunderstand me: I am not advocating the widespread use of vague pronouns; just last week I was reading poems for a class and I wrote in the margin of one: Who is the you? Yes, it happens, but there's no cause for hysteria or even mild concern on the subject of this bacteria infiltrating and destroying vital nerve tissue in American poetry. Mr. Sterling goes further. He says: "More to the point, I've often felt that the use of 'you' is somewhat accusatory and condemning in the first place—a literary quality perhaps inherited from Puritan sermonizing—and that such accusation turns readers away." I'd like to look at what I consider one of the greatest cases of the ill-defined you in English literature: the lines written by John Keats in his manuscript of *The Cap and Bells*, lines often printed with the title "This Living Hand."

> This living hand, now warm and capable
> Of earnest grasping, would, if it were cold
> And in the icy silence of the tomb,
> So haunt thy days and chill thy dreaming nights
> That thou wouldst wish thine own heart dry of blood
> So in my veins red life might stream again,
> And thou be conscience-calm'd—see here it is—
> I hold it towards you.

Surely there is no greater accusatory poem in existence. And sure enough we have to ask, *Who is the you?* It *used* to be believed that this poem was addressed to Fanny Brawne, Keats's sweetheart, but no one in their right mind thinks of Fanny when they read the poem, and to say "I hold it towards you, Fanny" is ridiculous. Perhaps it is a friend, or his brother George, or contemporary readers, or future readers, or contemporary critics. Or could it be Keats's own double, scribe within a scribe? The poem is nothing but a gigantic, disembodied hand pointing a finger at someone. That finger is a magnet and a conductor: it reaches out to the vague, ill-defined you like God reaching within an inch of Adam, and it charges the reader with all the responsibility in the world: go figure these things out for yourself, while you still have blood in your veins. Indeed, the lines are now thought of as being merely a passage Keats intended to use in some future poem: in other words, he himself had no idea who the you was or would be. At one point, Mr. Sterling in his essay says, "What I'm suggesting is that a poet cannot elicit an authentic response on a reader's part through the use of what is in fact false or fake." False or fake *what*? I thought our business was to make things up, you know, create them. I thought that was real. I thought I could *experience the fictive*. I thought figurative language was based on a ruse. I thought the twentieth century in particular—or at the very least Wallace Stevens and the Republic of France—had destroyed this notion of irreality, once and for all. I guess I was wrong. I guess I was just being sentimental, to love Keats's poem so much and not even know who the you was, which brings me to my second subject, sentimentality. It has been my privilege and pleasure to share the company of the other poet-teachers in the evening, and I thought you might be interested in what they talk about when they get together informally. They talk about cats. They exchange cat stories and show each other photographs of their cat-pets. I can't think of anything more sentimental than to own a cat, but that's only because I personally abhor them, though I am willing to admit that I am particularly fond of *kittens*, a form of cat even more sentimental than the real thing. I have noticed that when a cat has kittens, my friends give away the kittens and keep the cat. Which has always baffled me: in the same situation, I would give the cat away and keep the kittens. Which is more sentimental? A long-standing, associative relationship with a cat, a relationship of nuance and memory, the language—if you can call it that—of shared experience, or my own attachment to something that is more like a symbol, the feeling I have when I hold a kitten that here is something that has acquired a PhD in cuteness? When the late American novelist John Gardner defined sentimentality as "causeless emotion," he must have been thinking about kittens. But it seems to me the effect of an image in a poem often acts like a kitten: we are expected to go "*ah*" deep down in our interior sphere, and to slightly elevate ourselves in relation to the world, as if the soul were a beach ball. The kitten is a central image in Hart Crane's poem "Chaplinesque."

CHAPLINESQUE

We make our meek adjustments,
Contented with such random consolations
As the wind deposits
In slithered and too ample pockets.

For we can still love the world, who find
A famished kitten on the step, and know

Recesses for it from the fury of the street,
Or warm torn elbow coverts.

We will sidestep, and to the final smirk
Dally the doom of that inevitable thumb
That slowly chafes its puckered index toward us,
Facing the dull squint with what innocence
And what surprise!

And yet these fine collapses are not lies
More than the pirouettes of any pliant cane;
Our obsequies are, in a way, no enterprise.
We can evade you, and all else but the heart:
What blame to us if the heart live on.

The game enforces smirks; but we have seen
The moon in lonely alleys make
A grail of laughter of an empty ash can,
And through all sound of gaiety and quest
Have heard a kitten in the wilderness.

In a letter Crane wrote to William Wright in 1921, Crane explicitly states what he meant by the kitten: "Poetry, the human feelings, the 'kitten,' is so crowded out of the humdrum, rushing, mechanical scramble of today that the man who would preserve them must duck and camouflage for dear life to keep himself from annihilation." The poem may be sentimental, but Crane insists that if we fail to be moved by the kitten, something is terribly wrong. And when you think about it, poets always want us to be moved by *something*, until in the end, you begin to suspect that a poet is someone who is moved by *everything*, who just stands in front of the world and weeps and laughs and laughs and weeps (the mysteries, said Aristotle, are the saying of many ridiculous and many serious things). I've been using Gardner's definition of sentimental—causeless emotion, that is, indulgence of more emotion than seems warranted by the stimulus—for many years in teaching students why their sentimental poems don't work, and in explaining to myself why my own sentimental poems don't work. Until one day I realized that *causeless emotion* was an even better definition of *poetry*. In fact it is almost a paraphrase of Baudelaire's statement that poets possess "the ability of being vividly interested in things, even those that appear most trivial." To veer back to the poem "Chaplinesque" by Crane—and one has to remember that when this poem was written Chaplin was, though phenomenally popular, not yet enshrined as the master of high art that he is today—the very name Chaplin evokes the dark suit we recognize immediately as the veil, the very image, of sentimentality—and how curious that the suit is not all that different from the dark uniform of the policeman who chases and thwarts him, his shadow, the underside of sentimentality, the very cliché of unfeelingness, oppression, the thumb coming down on the tail of the rat (or is it a cat?), on the tails of the faux-tux topcoat. In fact, they are doubles, and it is all a marvelous play of mistaken identity, misplaced sympathy, and counterpoint, the movement that attempts to confer respectability on frivolity and frivolity on respectability. It's like those women who sell makeup in the department stores: the ones who wear white lab coats in an attempt to take seriously the great fun of painting your face. Poets do the same thing. One views them as either "custodians of pointless and absurd traditions" or as "custodians of the highest form of human expression." It's perfectly natural to waffle between the two: without perceptual, as well as emotional, counterpoint, none of us could survive. Keats said only one thing was necessary to write good poetry: a feeling for light and shade. I like that he had the sense to call it one thing, and not two things. In Wallace Stevens, it is his "*passion* for *restraint*." Speaking of Stevens, who has been almost deified in American letters, I came across a poem by Anna Akhmatova which reads exactly as though it were written by Stevens's wife. It offers a succinct and excellent criticism of the man.

HE LOVED . . .

He loved three things in life:
Evensong, white peacocks
And old maps of America.
He hated it when children cried,

He hated tea with raspberry jam
And women's hysterics.
... And I was his wife.

The man in this poem is chided for being sentimental, but
note how the female speaker doesn't hesitate to use equally sen-
timental images to evoke her side of the situation. And notice
how the very preoccupations she is chiding him for, the beau-
tiful, quiet things listed in the beginning, work as beautiful
quiet things in the poem: I think it is marvelous how what is
ridiculed enriches the poem and is part of its body. Note the
white peacock, a purely silent, visual image, yet echoed a sec-
ond time in the word *hysterics*, mindful of that animal's pierc-
ing cry, a cry Stevens himself ponders in more than one poem.
The revolutionist Russian poet Mayakovsky publicly said of
Akhmatova: "Anna Akhmatova's indoor intimacy ... what
meaning [has it] for our harsh and steely age? ... Of course, as
literary landmarks, as the last remnants of a crumbling order,
[her poems] will find their place in the pages of histories of lit-
erature, but for us, for our age, they are pointless, pathetic and
comic anachronisms." Yet Lily Brik, Mayakovsky's mistress for
many years, said that whenever he was in love he read Akhma-
tova, quoting her from morning till night! Nostalgia, which
evokes sentimentality, belongs exclusively to *culture*. Because
it belongs to the idea of progress and change and the idea of ac-

cumulation, accretion and storage. Only highly developed cultures foster feelings of nostalgia. The revolutionists must stop for orangeade. As Stevens says in his poem by the same name ("The Revolutionists Stop for Orangeade"), "This must be the vent of pity, / Deeper than a truer ditty." Prince Genji, the title character in Lady Murasaki's eleventh-century Japanese novel, the first novel ever written, sadly remembers the perfumes and brocades of his youth and laments the loss of craftsmanship in the present—that is, the year 1022. "Sentimentality will always be man's first revolt against development" (Peter Høeg). By development I'm not talking about Exxon; I'm talking about growth and change and death of any kind. I have no doubt but that one day Exxon will be someone's cherished memory. In regards to sentimentality, it seems to me you are damned if you do and damned if you don't. As I speak, blood is coursing through our bodies. As it moves away from the heart it *marches* to a ¾ or ¼ beat and it's arterial blood, reoxygenated, assertive, active, progressive, optimistic. When it reaches our extremities and turns toward home—the heart—well, it's nostalgic, it's venous blood (as in veins), it's tired, wavelike, rising and falling, fighting against gravity and inertia, and it moves to the beat of a waltz, a ¾ beat, a little off, really homesick now, and full of longing. When we first write our poems, how arterial they seem! And when we go back to them, how venous they seem! I recently got a letter from a friend. She wrote: "I have written a dozen poems since returning. I gave a little reading of half of them. People were encouraging. Wanted copies. Wanted to know when I'd make a book of them. But now, I look at them and they look like handkerchiefs. Something I needed to blow my nose in, wipe some tears with, with a little lace at the edges and my initials in the corner. Poetry is so weird." She's right. On both counts. "Mistrust of poetry has a long history," writes Donald Hall, and he's right, too—from Plato's *Republic*, where poets are banished from the Republic because everyone knows they could never be *reasonable*, to Nietzsche's oft-quoted "The poets lie too much," to Robert Hass's essay "Families and Prisons," which he delivered as the annual Hopwood Lecture at the University of Michigan in 1991, and in which he decides, having read all the previous Hopwood lectures by poets (such as W. D. Snodgrass and Denise Levertov), that "the first two-thirds of any lecture on poetry by a poet is likely to be more or less indiscreet self-praise; the final third is apt to deal with the supreme importance of poetry to human civilization." From Coleridge's notebooks in 1796, "Poetry— excites us to artificial feelings—makes us callous to real ones," to the Polish novelist Witold Gombrowicz's extraordinarily wonderful essay called "Against Poets," a long invective in which, after asserting that no one in their right mind under-stands a poem when it is read aloud (think of the Crane poem), he says: "If there is a storm of applause at a [recital], it does not necessarily mean that each of the clapping persons was fasci-nated. One timid applause provokes another—mutually exciting themselves until finally there arises a situation in which each person has to adjust himself internally to the collective madness. Everybody 'behaves' as if he were enthralled although no one is ever 'really' enthralled to this extent." Yes, the mistrust of poetry has a long history, for a variety of reasons, but they all come down to sentiment and invention over fact and truth. Figurative language is suspicious. *Pinnacled dim in the intense inane.* One of my favorite lines in all of poetry, but what does it *mean*? If Shelley is talking about a star in outer space, why doesn't he use the word *immense*? If he is referring to Promethean man, the paradoxes and trials of self-consciousness compacted inside the human skull, couldn't he be more specific? The words are spoken, in *Prometheus Unbound*, by "the Spirit of the Hour," yet what is the spirit of the hour for a poet but language itself? Shelley can't be any clearer because he is clearly attached, sentimentally, to language. Take Hart Crane and Dylan Thomas. Oh! The beauty of those sounds! Even though their main position seems to be one of interchangeableness or substitution: switch two descriptive lines from any given poems by one of these men and see if it makes any difference. And this is great stuff! Why is it that all the great stuff is never in keeping with what you are always told: don't be sentimental; every word must be exact, fitting, proper only to its singular place in a particular poem. Let's face it, poets are *expected* to be sentimental, since no one ever thinks of using their services except on the occasions of birth, marriage, and death, when one might be asked to read something suitable, that is, sentimental. And the French have a phrase for the love-life that makes possible at least two of these occasions: *the sentimental life*. When anyone asks me how my love-life is, I cringe. When my friend from Paris, M. Guy, asks me how is my sentimental life, I am delighted by the phrase—it opens a whole new set of possibilities; I'm thinking of Flaubert's title *Sentimental Education*, a term used to signify the series of heart-attachments and -unattachments from which one learns so much in a life. But obviously, I have committed the gravest essayistic grievance—I've been talking and talking and haven't even bothered to define sentimentality except to say that one man once called it "causeless emotion." In one way, causeless emotion reminds me of melancholy: when we have sorrows without a name. And Pablo Neruda warns us: "We must not overlook melancholy, the sentimentalism of another age, the perfect impure fruit whose marvels have been cast aside by the mania for pedantry: moonlight, the swan at dusk, 'my beloved,' are, beyond question, the elemental and essential matter of poetry. He who would flee from bad taste is riding for a fall." The word *sentimental*, for me, has something vague about it, too. It is based on the word *sentiment*, which comes from the Latin verb *to feel*. In other words, personal experience, one's own feeling, including physical feeling—sensation—and also mental feeling—emotion. A thought or reflection colored by or proceeding from emotion—an *emotional thought*. You begin to see the two-fold nature of the word itself: both thought and feeling. Even when we hear the word *sentiment*, and especially the word *sentimental*, there's the *sen* of sensuous, the *mental* of mind. When the word *sentimental* first came to us from the French in the middle of the eighteenth century, it was used in a favorable sense, that of possessing the most refined aesthetic emotion, exhibiting exquisite taste, expressing love but also intellectual idealism: if you wanted to convey a favorable impression of someone you just met, you would say, "Mr. Meyers is a sentimental man." But it didn't take long—a mere century—for the change to occur, so that by the middle of the nineteenth century if you wanted to convey that someone was full of nonsense, insincere and mawkish, you would say, "Mr. Meyers is a sentimental man." Now these dates are interesting: they more or less coincide with the age of Romanticism, which ended around 1832, and it is in 1837—in other words, *very* shortly thereafter—that we see the word start its rapid downward slide. Things changed, and as is always the case, what was ordinary, or even "of the moment," puts on the cloak, *for better or for worse*, of nostalgia. The ultimate definition of poetry for the Romantics was given by Wordsworth, but the everlasting pity is, his definition is always quoted out of context: "Poetry is the spontaneous overflow of powerful feelings." But the sentence went on, there was a comma after "feelings," followed by: "and though this be true, poems to which any value can be attached were never produced on any variety of subjects but by a man who, being possessed of more than usual organic sensibility, had also thought long and deeply." In other words, they are both arterial and venous. They give pleasure—or put a lump in our throats—*and they make us think.* As Robin Behn tells her students: "I want more than poignant stories." If your teachers suggest that your poems are sentimental, that is only the half of it. Your poems probably need to be even *more* sentimental. Don't be less of a flower, but could you be more of a stone at the same time? Could you have sympathic feelings in more than one direction? And can you think at the same time? From childhood, each of us operates under dual impulses—one toward safety (be earnest and diligent, do a good job, please others) and one toward danger (take risks! be courageous! damn them all!). Though fear of freedom is an entanglement in increasingly unimportant decisions—*should I use chiasmus in my work?*—fear of security also retards. This is Marianne Moore describing Edna St. Vincent Millay, who had given a reading at the Brooklyn Academy: "She was very romantic, had a long velvet cloak and gold slippers. Did it well. Then she read her piece about that dead kitten in a shoebox, covered with fleas. I was quite dismayed, felt affronted." How confusing it all is! A sentimental Miss Millay writes a poem about a dead kitten covered with fleas in a shoebox, and the unsentimental Miss Moore feels affronted, feels for the poor kitty and remembers how she buried her own kitten: under roses and white clematis, in "a fragrant grave." These two women are complex figures:

"No image can replace the intuition [of being], but many diverse images, borrowed from very different orders of things, may, by the convergence of their action, direct consciousness to the precise point where there is a certain intuition to be seized." That's the philosopher Henri Bergson, and it is quite close to Ezra Pound's explanation of image as "that which presents an intellectual and emotional complex in an instant of time." Insofar as they attempt to do this, all images are sentimental, or attempt to be sentimental, in the dual nature of that word.

For a long time I have been noticing the trend in advertising to be "poetic," both in imagery and copy, such as those Nike ads that go on and on, or the Guess ads, and Ralph Lauren "chapbooks" that employ only images, or—of particular interest to me—those ads that bandy the word *poetry* and its derivations, or quote lines from real poems, as if the very mention of poetry quadrupled a company's power to increase its capital gains. THE POETRY OF KNITS. The poetry of knits: just what *is* the poetry of knits? Well, for starters, I concede that a poem ought to be well-knit. But knit clothing usually implies *comfortable* clothing and a good poem is seldom comfortable; either it vanquishes us with anguish or electrifies us with ecstasy or makes us pause and consider a new sense of the world or unravels us altogether, but never does it make us feel comfortable in the fashion of these ads. But wait. Perhaps it *frees us* (like comfortable clothing) to feel all kinds of things. Perhaps it frees us to feel sentimental, creates a context in which we can be moved. These ads baffle me. And what about Odysseus's Penelope, who weaves by day and unravels by night? I begin to see that poetry has everything in the world to do with knits. That there is, after all, such a thing as "the poetry of knits." But wearing the clothing in the ads will not bring you one iota closer to it. Why are there no books in the ad? I note only the following: a magazine, a newspaper, a camera, a rocking chair, and a dog. The presence of water. Shoelaces. And the copy: "Introspection comes naturally in the warmth of a relaxed ribbed sweater." But *why*? I daresay we are in the presence of the sentimental, where an object—a sweater—is linked to a feeling—reverie. (And we can't forget it's autumn, which in poetry is a pretty good stand-in for reverie.) Why doesn't it work? The rest of the copy is made up of quotations by well-known women writers—May Sarton, Emily Brontë, Toni Morrison—and I suppose these phrases about *dreaming*, the *inner world*, *thoughts*, and *emotions* are supposed to be stand-ins for whole poems. And the models are supposed to be stand-ins for *you*. I want to say sentimentality seldom works when there are stand-ins, but I know better: I know images and metaphors are often rhetorical stand-ins. Why doesn't any of this make sense to me? I know it's wrong, meaning I sense there's something false about it, but I can't "prove it" without bringing poetry down in the same swoop; could it be because it's all true? Jane Austen used to write *How true!* underneath poems she was not fond of. This ad is telling the truth, but it's an obvious one. If it is, as Aristotle says, "the mark of a poet to see a connection between apparently incongruous things," then these copywriters have seen a connection between *congruous* things—leisure and reverie, and, as we shall see, beauty and object, taste and class, money and symbol. There is a New Glass Gallery ad that features a line by Keats, the famous opening of *Endymion*, an early work: "A thing of beauty is a joy forever." One presumes forever means both before and after death, though it's hard to imagine a broken glass preserved and lingering in our memory, offering the "lasting magic" of the ad-promise. But glass *is* among the most perishable of things, and Keats might have approved. Books of poetry are also often "on sale," especially Keats's, but the world prefers a goblet to an urn, and who can blame them? I don't think there's anything inherently wrong with any of these ads, other than that no one reads them; imagine the man who would read the ad featuring "A thing of beauty is a joy forever," put down the newspaper, and stare at the ceiling in contemplation of the words. Let's look at the goblet offered by Waterford Crystal: "It is like poetry, sensuous and flowing, filled with light and mysterious shadows. Burnished and incandescent, an object that can bewilder time and exist in another realm. Reflections of Venetian palaces and French bistros pass by. 'Hold me,' it says, 'I have things to tell you.'"

Now, at first you may balk, but is there among you one who would not be proud to have at least part of that as a blurb on your first or next book? I also want to point out that the copywriter has done a good job. Note the counterpoint between "Venetian palaces" and "French bistros"—far better than if he had said "Venetian palaces and French castles." And notice the mention of both light and shadow—very Keatsian. How far off can the copywriter be? And the anthropomorphism of the speaking goblet! That's a very nice touch. "Hold me" (pick up the glass). "I have things to tell you" (bring it to your lips). The only thing missing is the human being who is drinking from this enchanted vessel: How did he or she acquire the glass? Where do they keep it? How often do they use it? What does it *say*, for god's sake, besides, "I have something to say"? Does it say "Going to Him! Happy letter!" or "I hear America snowing" or "Life, friends, is boring"? If only the ad *persisted* in its sentimentality—it would be well on its way to becoming a poem or story. A Guide to Poetic Living is what all these ads seem to offer, and they would be successful, I think, if there *were* a guide, but not even poetry itself is a reliable guide.

OUTSIDE

Oh, we know what goes on or someone will give
us the real dirt. Quite a few were there
at the cabinet table or in the locker room

and heard direct. They know what was said and where
the power was. Not that someone else
—and he might have his reasons—also there
might not tell us different and be right but then
it isn't simple and keeps us occupied
not just with now but with ancient history
while elsewhere it happens if happens is what it does
and I don't think so and I don't know what goes on.

WILLIAM BRONK

Sentimentality is more than the object of our affection—it's the object of our *invention*. Alas, I cannot find my favorite ad, a full-page colored ad for a luxury automobile—I think it was a Jaguar—which printed in a Latinate font a phrase of Coleridge's prose on the symbol of objects: "A symbol is characterized by the translucence of the eternal through and in the temporal." What myths do you want to perpetuate? What myths do you want to destroy? In the era of Prince Genji, eleventh-century Japan, poems were used to begin and end conversations between lovers, and in all forms of letter-writing; even as I am aware that such a guide for poetical living was available to a mere 10 percent of the population, those who constituted the inner circle of court life, that is, those who were literate and of means, I have always found these things astonishingly wonderful. Then why do I balk at the fact that in late-twentieth-century

America, poetry is used to sell commodities? After all, not all the commodities are luxuries—lead crystal and Jaguars to be sure, but not running shoes or soft, comfortable clothing. Aren't I involving myself in a double standard? Which era is exemplary, which absurd? Which the kitten and which the cat? What right have I, a sentimental poet, to point a finger at anyone? So in the end, I do not know how I feel about these ads.

We are human beings. Our expressions are always inadequate, often pitiful. Poetry is sentimental to begin with. To write a sentimental poem is an act of redundancy. That is all I can say to my students. But even in poems that are not doubly sentimental in this way, it is terribly insufficient how an image, a crushed corsage *or* an M16, cannot recreate or give more than momentary value to the event it evokes in the mind of its retainer. All we can say in defense of our insane tribulations is that they were an act of love—a supremely sentimental act—an act of causeless emotion—that made us commit embarrassing gestures. Our vision is so distorted that, like Proust's character Swann, we are in love with something we don't like, can't trust, and have nothing in common with. Perhaps I should not say "we," lest we miss the emergency exit in our confusion over pronouns; I will therefore revert to the staircase of "I." I have wasted my life, I have wasted it gladly, remorsefully, willingly, and in the full knowledge there were many things that would not have been different, or would have been better off, had they been left unsaid. Eventually, in every poet's life, there must come the recognition of the possibility of *unhitching*. I take the word *unhitching* from Claude Lévi-Strauss's *Tristes Tropiques*, an anthropology book that, for better or for worse, changed the views of Western civilization in the twentieth century. Here is the passage I have in mind:

> The possibility, vital for life, of *unhitching*, which consists ... in grasping, during the brief intervals in which our species can bring itself to interrupt its hive-like activity, the essence of what it was and continues to be, below the threshold of thought and over and above society; in the contemplation of a mineral more beautiful than all our creations; in the scent that can be smelt at the heart of a lily and is more imbued with learning than all our books; or in the brief glance, heavy with patience, serenity and mutual forgiveness, that, through some involuntary understanding, one can sometimes exchange with a cat.

ON THEME

Themes dominate contemporary American society, and our predominantly Christian culture has been perfecting them for more than a century, whether you are part of that culture or not, whether you like it or not. After hearts shot through with arrows, we have bunnies followed by a warlike fire in the sky, then ghosts, turkeys to honor more ghosts, and a baby born in a barn who is not yet a ghost but also a ghost, for whom we drag trees inside where they do not belong. Holidays are the thematic passing of time, and you don't have to live in a temperate zone or look at a calendar to tell what time of year it is; you have only to enter a store, or a school, or a hospital, or a post office, and check out the images and icons. Recently a board of concerned parents formed to protest the celebration of Halloween in public schools, citing it as satanic, reverberating insidiously in the psyches of young children. Holidays in fact have their origins in cults; I mean, they are based on pagan rituals, most of which were later, in the first century AD, assimilated by early Christians. Assimilated and transformed, often beyond recognition.

And the more I think about theme, the more I am drawn to the idea that theme is always an extrapolation, a projection, an extension or expansion of an original idea, if such a thing as an original idea exists. To extrapolate means to arrive at conjectural knowledge concerning an unknown area. That is, to take what is known or has been experienced and project that knowledge into an area not known or experienced so as to arrive at knowledge of the unknown by inference. But sometimes we seem to extrapolate so strangely that it is the supposedly known source itself that becomes unknown, becomes unrecognizably distorted and weird. In such cases, the original idea seems not to have expanded but to have shrunk, a pitiful petrification of itself.

American suburban subdivisions are quite concerned with theme. My parents live in relative opulence on Madura Road, named after a city in India, and to get to their house in Tiger Point Village I have to go a long way down Ganges Trail, past Tibet Place and Calcutta Drive. The idea of India—and the miscalculated oddity of Tibet in the middle of it—gives a distinctive unity to the neighborhood and has become its signature, but of course it is a strange extrapolation; the community bears no resemblance to India that I can think of, either on or beneath the surface. What is theme? Theme is, simply, a subject or topic—for our purposes, of discourse or artistic representation, including architecture and design. For instance, my theme is theme. But my *real* theme is poetry, though I will not be mentioning it much. Because, since you are poets, I assume you think metaphorically. Isn't that the way you read? True or false: the subject or topic of a poem is never really its subject or topic. Robert Frost never wrote a nature poem. He said that. Meaning: there's more to me than trees and birds. Meaning: there's more to trees and birds and I know that, so that means there's more to me, too.

One of the ways you can tell there's more to people than you might think is to go to their houses. If they have a lot of books, well, that means something. But don't just look at the books, look at the way the books are organized on the shelves, for there are many different ways to do this. Two or so years ago I read in a magazine that you could hire an interior decorator to come to your house and arrange your books by color in such a way as to coordinate with the color scheme of the particular room they were in. Of course I laughed out loud at this unintelligent absurdity. But a few weeks ago I found myself alone in my living room, staring at my book shelves and imagining the books arranged by color, and I grew very, very fond of the idea. It would be a whole new way of thinking about books. Where is my Isabelle Eberhardt? With the blue books. Presently my books are arranged by genre, which is a kind of subject, as if theme were form: poetry, fiction, history, biography, the natural sciences, art books, philosophy, criticism, etc, etc. Most libraries are organized on this principle. But I have friends whose books are arranged alphabetically, by author; libraries also incorporate this principle within the other principle. And then I know someone whose books are arranged by sex: men in one section, women in another, gays and lesbians in a third. If you are thinking this is an insult to gays, all I can say is the owner of this particular library is gay. And some people shelve their books, simply, in the order in which they have been read. Which is perhaps the most personal and individual way it can be done, which goes to show there is no organizing principle to the personal and individual. There is of course a principle at work, I have just stated it, but it's not one you would recognize if you looked at the books—you would be looking for one of the other principles. But *never*, in my life, have I seen a library organized by theme. When I stand in front of my shelves and try to organize my books by theme, I am at a loss. First I will have to reread three-fourths of my library, paying special attention to theme, and then I will have to buy three copies of each book so that it might fit into all the theme-sections to which it belongs. Where do I put *War and Peace*? *The Tibetan Book of Living and Dying*? *The Complete Plays of William Shakespeare*? Do I saw my Stevens in half? I am sincerely confused by all this. Any attempt to divide my books by theme is completely arbitrary. In fact, it strikes me as no different, perhaps worse, than dividing them by color. I am led to believe theme is absolutely meaningless in the long run. But part of me cannot believe I just said that. Auden said a poem should be more interesting than anything that might be said about it. If you take the theme out of a poem and talk about that theme, there should still be some residual being left in the poem that goes on ticking, something like, why not say it, *color*, something that has an effect on your central nervous system. It is not what a poem says with its mouth, it's what a poem does with its eyes. Have you looked recently at the classified ads in any poetry trade rag? The call for poems is astounding. Anthologies want poems from *you* and they want poems from *me*. This is only a partial listing of the themes that are in demand, like certain toys at Christmas, and this list is not invented by me for my own purposes of persuasion, but extracted verbatim: AIDS, California expatriates, quilts, victims of child abuse, dogs, automobiles, sailing, incest, condoms, those who have known and loved African American men who have been incarcerated, childbirth, spiritual experiences among lesbians, New Jersey, poems by women in response to poems by men, and, my favorite, a call for poems for the "Unique Anthology"—they want "any theme, but especially interested in Sweet Revenge, Fish Out of Water, Narrow Escape, Reversal of Fortune."

Something is terribly, terribly, terribly wrong here. Isn't AIDS trivialized by being on this list? Isn't childbirth? Aren't African American men who have been incarcerated? Aren't dogs? Isn't sailing? What's being trivialized here is poetry. When the New Critics emphasized "reading as thematizing" little did they know to what extent their thrust would be extrapolated by poets in the twenty-first century. Although the dic-

tionaries define theme as subject or topic, the new critical defi-
nition of theme—and I take this from a glossary of literary
terms continuously in print from 1941 to 1971—and now out of
print—is that theme is "the basic *idea* or *attitude* behind a
work." The key word here, I think, is *behind*, because to an iro-
nist—and all postmoderns are ironists—there is no behind. Of
course Shakespeare was an ironist, since Timon of Athens lifts
the silver lid off the banquet platter and—lo and behold—*noth-
ing's* there, and Melville was an ironist, since he wrote: "By vast
pains we mine into the pyramid; by horrible gropings we come
to the central room; with joy we espy the sarcophagus; but we
lift the lid—and no body is there!" Today we mine many poems
with similar results—the themes on the surface pass as ad-
mirably deep embodiments of the human condition, but once
we get inside we discover something *worse* than nothing: we
discover a mess of wires, we discover the android that theme
has become. Is it any surprise to discover that poets themselves
are becoming androids?

Androids are supposed to imitate human beings. The best
thing about the best androids is that they are indistinguishable
from human beings. When a poet is said to imitate his or her
self it implies that his or her signature—a repeated, recogniza-
ble style—has grown too familiar; the instantly recognizable
personality is not a personality, it is a commodified cult. Hav-
ing such a thought, one is seized with a gripping fear: Is this go-
ing to happen to *me*? Has this already happened to *me*? Young

poets are always talking about voice: Do I have a voice? How can I get a voice? What is a voice? How long will getting a voice take? And then, voilà: Now that I have a voice, I am terribly depressed by my voice, having a voice has kinda made me a robot, hasn't it? The fear is amplified not out of personal paranoia but out of a collective one: we live in a culture where *no one* can escape being instantly recognizable. No purdah for us! In a culture based on the proliferation of choice, even one's outward appearance, whether or not you are conscious of it, whether or not you care, is interpreted by the public as a decision. Please do not misunderstand me: you may not have *had* a choice, but the public is going to assume you made one. The political implications of this are many, and would be best discussed by a political analyst, which I am not. What I am equipped to discuss is Polartec. I recently acquired my first article of clothing made out of Polartec. I like the fabric for its texture, that it's soft, warm, light, and washable. But to me it carries with it connotations of an outdoorsy, athletic lifestyle —since it was originally developed for these activities—and I am not an outdoorsy, athletic type, because I believe, stupidly, that this will disenhance whatever intellectual qualities I may possess. I choose not to be associated with L.L. Bean, the clothing manufacturer whose first appearance in American poetry was, by the way, in a poem by Robert Lowell. So I found myself in a quandary I finally resolved by choosing a *bathrobe* made out of Polartec; I could enjoy the qualities of the fabric I liked without having to be seen wearing it in public. While wearing my new robe I was given a copy of the October 2, 1995, *New Yorker*—a magazine I refuse to subscribe to but secretly read—and there, in an article by Susan Orlean on the difficulty of dressing in a seasonless urban society, exacerbated by temperature control in the forms of air-conditioning and central heating, was my synthetic bathrobe and the synthetic person wearing it:

> Take polar fleece for instance. Polar fleece is a plush, spongy, totally artificial material that weighs nothing and conveys no quality of warmth or coolness; in fact, you can wear it in the most bitter weather or in the hottest heat. Polar fleece looks neither flimsy and light nor hearty and warm. It has no historical, cultural, or physical association with a place, a season, a society, or any living thing. It is the first existential fabric—eminently useful, meaningless, dissociated and weird.

My god, I thought, it could be Dean Young talking about poetry! I recognized the same themes everywhere, as they overlapped and cross-referenced themselves ad nauseam.

I decided I needed to find an original idea, something pure and spare and untainted, and since it was a glorious autumn weekend in October, I decided to visit the Shakers. I visited several Shaker villages, most notably Hancock Shaker Village in Pittsfield, Massachusetts, the town where Herman Melville

wrote most of *Moby-Dick* while looking out at one of the Berk-
shire Mountains that is shaped like a humpback whale. Of
course there are no Shakers living in Hancock Village, but as it
is a thriving nonprofit historical foundation the original build-
ings are admirably restored and kept up in tip-top Shaker style,
and a load of family activities are daily promoted which suc-
cessfully attract families who come to see the architecture, the
weaving, the chair-making, the sheep-shearing, the herb-gath-
ering, and the pure, simple, unadorned, and stunning interi-
ors. If there is a Shaker theme, it is simplicity. Simplicity of life
and simplicity of style. The Shakers were celibate communi-
ties of men and women for whom work was a form of prayer—
hands to work, hearts to God—but these touring villages are
baffling to me: I asked a young couple, wearing Polartec pull-
overs and carrying their three-year-old daughter, why they re-
turned every October for the fall festival of activities. "Because
it's inspiring," they said, "for us to see the clean lines of spiri-
tual space, and fun for our daughter, who loves animals. It is the
perfect family activity." Now if it were 1880 and they had ar-
rived on the premises to join the community, this is what would
have happened: Their child would be taken from them to live
with the other children and be educated in a classroom with-
out a globe. The husband and wife would then be separated
and lodged, respectively, on the east and west sides of the main
compound's second story, down the center of which runs a
polished wooden corridor, down the center of which runs, ac-

cording to my guide, an invisible line, like the equator, a line every man and woman was acutely aware of, since they lived on only one side of it for the rest of their lives. You could not cross the line, but you could freely see the other side—the other sex—in all their comings and goings. Is there anywhere else in the world a monastic situation quite like this? Where all temptation is to be (1) shunned and (2) in full and frontal view? In a Shaker community all letters from the outside world were read first by the elders, who edited them and then read them aloud— any indiscreet remarks and/or references to the outside world removed—to the entire community, so that Jane sat in her beautiful straight-back chair, designed so that an angel might come and sit on it, and heard for the first time a letter from her father. 'Tis a gift to be simple; 'tis a gift to be free. I do not deny the beauty of Shaker design, the genius of their marketing skills (the Shakers were savvy realtors, businessmen, and exporters—best of all, they invented *pills*, which, in their *simplicity*, revolutionized the pharmaceutical world, and they produced the cherry-red cloak Little Red Riding Hood wore, and intricately patterned chair seats, colors and designs they themselves shunned but knew would *sell* well), nor do I deny the hard-won spiritual peace that many of them must have achieved. But I deny the present-day site its *theme* of family fun, I deny the special events scheduled for Mother's Day and Father's Day; none of them have anything to do with the original sensibility of the Shakers; it is a form of restatement devoid of everything that drove the original. Most visitors spend a day at the village, visiting all the buildings, the restaurant, the gift shop, and leave, village map in hand, without seeing the Shaker graveyard. Indeed, when I asked my guide directions to the graveyard she said, "But there's nothing to see!" And so I went. Across a field, over a footbridge, past a row of cornstalks, one turns and sees another empty field with a modest obelisk at its center. Here Lie the Shaker Dead—or something to that effect. At the beginning of this century, the elders decided to change the nature of Shaker burial and removed all of the individual headstones, using them for sidewalks, countertops, and ironing boards. Standing there one is confronted with the *real* Shaker theme—a simple, empty meadow full of the dead who have been stripped of their names, like the anonymous burying grounds of war, all individuals gone to a greater cause— which may be noble, and may be moving—but is *not* the theme of the Christmas-candle-dipping exhibition designed for liberal, New England families interested in individual integrity. By the way, nineteenth-century insane asylums also buried their dead without names—as if the deceased belonged to an anonymous collective insanity.

Which brings me to Las Vegas. Something similar to what has happened in Shaker villages is happening in the commercial district of Las Vegas; on the Strip, more and more hotels and casinos are being marketed toward safe, fun family visits— the kids can play in an acre of supervised video games while you hit the slots on the floor below; indeed, reference to the changes in Las Vegas are made at the end of the recent Scorsese film, *Casino*. The changes sadden me, for I am a devotee of Las Vegas as it was originally conceived—an ever-expanding, decentered, chaotic, instantly accessible space of pure thematic wonder: Caesars Palace, the old Moorish Aladdin, the volcanic Mirage, the *Kon-Tiki*ish Tropicana: Las Vegas is one of the finest examples of theme in America because it is itself and not a replication of itself, though its theme *is* replication and it replicates—as I think is true of any "genuine" theme— archetypes other than itself. It does so with a vengeance and a reverence, for Las Vegas is the uniquely American restatement of the Italian piazza. "Las Vegas is to the Strip what Rome is to the Piazza": one of the more famous assertions of the now-classic book *Learning from Las Vegas*, by the architects Robert Venturi, Denise Scott Brown, and Steven Izenour. Though "the image of the commercial strip is chaos," and that of a Shaker village order, the two operate under what I think are similar "pressures." The Strip in Las Vegas can be likened to the invisible line running down the Shaker living quarters; in the Shaker case, the possibility of chaos is not obvious but pervasive and underlying, and in the Vegas case, the possibility of order is not obvious but pervasive and underlying. To restate it: in one case we have order on the surface and chaos beneath, and in the other chaos on the surface and order beneath. In either case, as August Heckscher puts it, "Chaos is very near; its nearness, but its avoidance, gives the poetry its force."

In Las Vegas one gives in to temptation—that is what it is all about—drinking, eating, gambling, sex—but the situation is just as "artificial" and "unnatural" as celibacy among Shakers, because Las Vegas is just as far removed from the outside world, shuns the outside world, is nothing like the outside world. That's why people go there. In fact, the *real* invisible line separating chaos from order is not the Strip at all but the parameter of the town dividing Las Vegas from the desert, *the* landscape of spiritual imagination, birthplace of three of the world's major religions. Las Vegas gives the finger to the desert, and at the workaday cities of human endeavor beyond its horizons. The *undifferentiation* I see between Vegas and the Shaker village points to what the critic René Girard would call a mimetic association in which contraries disagree because they agree too much. This leads me to think about the ways in which imitation takes place, and how a direct obvious imitation often produces a sterile imitation because none of the original sensibilities are actually emulated, only a product-orientated spin-off, like Barbie's many clones. Interior designers are acutely aware of the perils of imitating a theme. Let's go back, again, to 1880. I want you to picture a genuine Victorian interior in all its stylistic eclecticism, for eclecticism was the driving sensibility behind the Victorian sense of decor, though in tasteless imitation this has been all but lost. Picture an over-stuffed sofa on small, polished claws, a round table beside it covered with a fringed shawl from India, a conglomerate of photographs and pillows, overlapping rugs, dark-shaded lamps, objects, both masculine and feminine, from around the world and reflecting the textures of that world, bibelots infused with sentimental value, tokens of experience, of travel; in other words the boundaries of Empire arranged around a *hearth*, a sense of center like a magnet attracting many odd filings, a sense of family, of home, of comfort, safety, and value—all determined by a cultural sense of privilege and power. Now imagine the same room reproduced in a contemporary home. It looks, simply, *Victorian*; its theme has become an instantly recognizable style, and in hasty summation—asked to pick two adjectives—we would probably call this *English* and *feminine*, possibly *romantic*. Its original idea has shrunk; any decent decorator would take one look and be bored: the room makes an established design statement with historical reference. But if you take the same room and refurnish it to its present overfilled state by mixing and matching a variety of periods and styles, careful to cover all the surfaces, hang three abstract paintings where one would do, use colors alien to the nineteenth century, but cluttering and comforting all the while, a designer might look at *you* and say *you* have a Victorian sensibility, and you might have some genuine understanding of the word's significance in the world of design.

After I returned from the Hancock Shaker Village, I was invited to a party with a theme. The invitation said, "You are invited to a Tex-Mex Fiesta." It was held outdoors, under a tent, and as the guests arrived the men were given sheriff's badges and sombreros, and the women were given Spanish mantillas —a square of black lace uplifted by a sequined piece of cardboard attached to a headband. Each table was decorated with cowbells, a small potted cactus, salt and pepper shakers in the shapes of boots, and the flatware was wrapped in red-and-white bandanas. Outside the tent the hills of Vermont rolled away in the distance, a state without the least resemblance to Texas or Mexico, a state that is now associated with the placid black-and-white dairy cow, an image that exploded on the theme market with undreamt-of success just at the time dairy farming was collapsing as a primary source of income for the state and the cows themselves were disappearing from the hillsides like stars at dawn. And I recently made several trips to midtown Manhattan, where a kind of urban renewal is taking place that alarms many native New Yorkers—the proliferation of theme restaurants in the form of Planet Hollywood, the Hard Rock Cafe, the Fashion Cafe, the Motown Cafe, the Jekyll and Hyde Club, and the Harley-Davidson Cafe. "A native New Yorker leaves the city he loves when he enters one of these places," laments one writer. I picked up a copy of *Architectural Digest* in a doctor's office and looked at photographs of Barbara Streisand's many homes, each one singularly devoted to a period theme: the star divides her time between an Early American country home, an Art Deco home, an Art Nouveau home, and a French Provincial home. There is a bar in Chicago where Bach and Vivaldi play in the background while Picassos and Kandinskys are projected in passing rapidity on the walls. Mismatched? Not when *Art* is the theme. And if this is too narrow a slice of art for you, picture that small café you sat in last week where they played the hottest jazz and had a traveling show of tribal totems on the wall. There is a tidal wave of theme in America. I live in a town of 17,000 people and eleven restaurants; twenty years ago only one restaurant was conscious of its theme—it was a fern bar replete with 1970s stained glass and spider plants, the first salad bar in town. Today there is not a single restaurant without a theme; to find one you have to drive twenty-five minutes into the country, and whenever I take anyone there they are usually disgusted. It's a small family-run family restaurant making and serving overcooked hearty meals, meat and potatoes, pies, doughnuts, milkshakes—and though it was always a country restaurant it never *thought* of itself as one. But the last time I went things had begun to change: the dirty white curtains had been replaced by calico, the bare walls filled with antique kitchen implements and plenty of pigs, cows, and cats. Evidently, it had gained a self-consciousness. Someone had said, "You have an identity—cash in on it." Art has always been aware of itself as art. Even the premise behind "found art" is that there has to be somebody who *finds it*, or it has to be put in a context that is art-conscious: a urinal in a museum. As far as I understand it, artists are trying very hard to be as inclusive as possible, to broaden consciousness so that there are fewer and fewer boundaries, lines of demarcation. High and low merge with the great middle. Everyone is self-conscious of having a signature; so what if there aren't an infinite number of hard-won styles; the next best thing is to join the camp closest to you. In fact, there don't seem to be any options in this tyranny of options, and no one can be blamed for having to choose between the Shakers and Vegas when it is your earthly right to have a choice and you have no choice but to choose between themes that are alarmingly similar. I don't have any answers. I'm lucky enough to occasionally be able to do something I love—write poems—and unlucky enough that what I love confuses and overwhelms me. Something stranger and stranger is getting closer and closer. I think again and again of a fragment the philosopher Wittgenstein wrote on a slip of paper: "It would almost be like settling how much a toss is to be worth by another toss." I pick up the morning paper and read that in Orlando—"home" of Disney World and Epcot—the powers that be are "turning their cloning skills closer to home." They have decided to build a theme park based on a rival Floridian destination—Key West. Now you don't have to drive the extra seven hours to visit Key West; you can stop in central Florida and visit Old Key West Resort. "The concept is a salute to Key

West," says a spokesman for SeaWorld, the investing developers. SeaWorld is owned by Anheuser-Busch. The new theme park will give tourists "the funky feel and funky colors" of Key West, while sparing them the real thing. The Disney Company is slated to begin another project near Orlando—something so close to home it *is* home. After years of building theme parks, they are building their masterpiece, an incorporated town named Celebration, where people can become permanent residents in what is promised to be a utopian community: 4,900 acres of small-town America circa 1940. The past is theme and in eight years 20,000 people will live there. You can live on a million-dollar estate, in a nice suburban home, a modest cottage, a nifty townhouse, or in a practical $650-a-month apartment, and you can choose from the following architectural styles: Classical, Colonial, Victorian, Coastal, Mediterranean, or French. Architects working on the project include Robert Stern, Philip Johnson, and Michael Graves; that's like saying Seamus Heaney, Czesław Miłosz, and John Ashbery. There will be a church and a school, a post office, a hospital, and a graveyard. There will be globes in the classrooms, and a teacher-training academy financed by Disney. The houses will be wired into a fiber-optic grapevine. I think the project will succeed because there is nothing quite like it—it is an original replica—offering prenuclear serenity governed by fiber-optic wizardry; but I think replicas of the replica—and they *will* follow—will probably fail. "Celebration is the most important thing happening in architecture," said, back in 1995, the Sterling Professor Emeritus of Art History at Yale University. "It marks a return of community. . . . Celebration grows out of the way people want to live—no question about it." Adding, "God, how I hate that name. It's really terrible."

Louise Bogan, in 1969, nearing the end of her life, after reviewing poetry for the *New Yorker* for thirty-eight years, was repelled by books with titles like *The Lice*, by W. S. Merwin. She wrote in confidence to a friend, "But really, Ruth, I've *had* it. No more pronouncements on lousy verse. . . . No more struggling *not* to be square." Poetry is, in so many ways—and I am not the first to say it—a young person's genre. Choice, and all its attendant energy, is characteristic of youth. It is before one chooses that one feels desire and longing without fulfillment, which gives an edge to any artistic endeavor. Galway Kinnell recently said in an interview that a young poet has so many choices but an old poet must simply endure his chosen life. Look at young Baudelaire's title "Invitation to the Voyage" and compare it to the older Stevens's title "The Rock." In my lifetime, I have believed that poetry, poetry from all periods and all cultures, has had only one theme, that of mutability.

Love and death, innocence and experience, praise and lament, the passing of time, appearance and reality, stability and instability; all these marked themes are nothing less—or more—than mutability. I see it in Egyptian songs and I see it in the work of Charles Bernstein. And, though I am embarrassed to say something so fundamental and obvious, mutability offers us no choice at all: we die, it is built into our wiring, like those batteries designed for obsolescence that so infuriate us consumers. I have nothing else to say about theme; the whole subject has begun to depress me, like the classified ads in poetry magazines. As Roland Barthes reminds us, Maupassant often ate lunch at the Eiffel Tower, because it was the only place in Paris from which the Eiffel Tower could not be seen. Where is the Eiffel Tower of poetry, and could we have lunch there?

ON SECRETS

Eight Beginnings, Two Ends

1

Everybody loves secrets—that's why you are here. And still you know, in your heart of hearts, in that secret place which is your own, that no secret will be revealed to you, not today, not yesterday, not tomorrow, not upon your deathbed, or in that last poem you chance to read or write or hear before they pull that winding-sheet over your head. And still we come and still we listen and crane our necks and cup our ears. And yet I know with absolute certainty that each of you, as you entered this room, passed through the doors, and found your seats, carried a secret inside you, as a child is carried in the womb. So let us go back to the womb, for we are born voyeurs. The sense of hearing is the first we acquire and the last we lose. Everyone knows, or should know, that a child inside the womb is sensitive to sounds outside the mother's body, and that a dying human in a comatose state can quite possibly hear everything that is being said by the people standing around him. I remember a pregnant friend singing softly all afternoon to her unborn daughter, because, as she put it, "John and I had a terrible fight last night and I think she's scared." I remember my brother, the last time he saw my mother, whose flesh rotted *before* she died, lifting his surgical mask and saying, "She stinks. I can't take the smell." And my arrogant, knowledgeable hand waving madly at him, pointing to her, pointing to my ear, a sign language for, "She might be able to hear you, don't say that!" When I think of that *now*, it strikes me as curious that we should be so concerned about purifying what the dying hear, while in our lives we don't think twice about saying embarrassing, hurtful, mean, painful things to the person standing in front of us with two perfectly good ears on either side of her head. Which brings me to another subject. Very often as a teacher and reader I encounter poems that *do not take my feelings into account*, and this is unacceptable to me! Every time I read a poem I am willing to die, insofar as I am surrendering myself to the mercy of someone else's speech, and I do not want to die in the presence of someone else's vile corruption of feeling. You are supposed to be preparing me for my death. Do not misunderstand me: rage, sadness, uncertainty, discomfort, awkwardness, resignation, and lament are subjects of a great many poems I am very willing to hear, as are poems of joy, surprise, delight, and tenderness, as are poems that renounce emotion in favor of a detached observation of the outer world or indulge only in an exploration of language itself, all of them poems of the wandering spirit in search of an unknown finality, in search of a secret. I want you to imagine for a moment something that is actually impossible to imagine—the unborn child in the womb perceiving through sound an outside world it has absolutely no experience of, no concept of, and no perception of except through sound. The experience of the fetal being is the experience of sound without sense; the fetal being is overhearing a secret, a true secret insofar as what it hears is not revealed as having a discernible meaning, and so is still *kept*, still remains a secret, all the while still being experienced, revealed, as sound, which is *not* hiding itself. So you might say our first "experience" of the world is of a secret. Our first experience of the world is that the world is a secret, that is, *it neither hides itself nor reveals itself.*

I was once such a child: I was twenty-four years old and someone took a phonograph needle and played for me the Brazilian soprano Bidú Sayão, an international opera star in the 1930s, '40s, and '50s. She found a lifelong friend in the composer Villa-Lobos, who once rose in the morning, took a piece of paper, and sketched the hills on the horizon. The outline or contour of those hills he then set onto a musical graph, and where the notes fell, he played them. After I believed this, a musician told me not a word of it was true, but I like it so much I continue to believe it. Whatever the case, I think Villa-Lobos understood the voice of things. In the aria of *Bachianus brasi-leiras no. 5*, Bidú Sayão persuaded Villa-Lobos to transcribe for her voice what had originally been a violin solo; an impromptu, experimental take was made in New York, in 1945, "just to hear how it would sound." It was never recut. Everyone in the studio knew, immediately, there was no need. The recording lasted seven minutes. First you hear Bidú Sayão sing the part of the violin, then you hear the violin, then you hear Bidú Sayão resing the melody, this time with her mouth completely *closed*—she is humming—and the last note you hear her sing, an octave's leap, was achieved with a completely closed mouth.

And this is a poem I found a few weeks ago by accident among my papers. I put it together when I was twenty years old. I say "put it together" because these were the circumstances: I was stuck in a house whose only book was a dictionary of the Native American Osage language. In the back of the book were prose paragraphs, in Osage, of some of the tribe's popular songs and legends, and, looking each word up in the dictionary one by one, I adapted several into English, my native tongue.

SONG OF SPEAKS-FLUENTLY

To have to carry your own corn far—
who likes it?
To follow the black bear through the thicket—

who likes it?
To hunt without profit, to return weary without anything—
who likes it?
You have to carry your own corn far.
You have to follow the black bear.
You have to hunt to no profit.

If not, what will you tell the little ones? What will you
    speak of?
For it is bad not to use the talk which God has sent us.
I am Speaks-Fluently. Of all the groups of symbols,
I am a symbol by myself.

Now what amazes me is that Speaks-Fluently was born, and
much later Villa-Lobos was born, and still later Bidú Sayão was
born, and later still I was born, and by some miracle I cannot
figure out, it was given to me to hear these voices, and all these
examples of a human life were speaking, and when I listened
carefully I could hear that they were speaking about speaking,
and when I listened carefully to them speaking about speaking
I could hear they were singing about listening. And that has
been a long journey for me, of listening. I used to think I wrote
because there was something I wanted to say. Then I thought,
"I will continue to write because I have not yet said what I
wanted to say"; but I know now I continue to write because I
have not yet heard what I have been listening to.

"I think I will do nothing for a long time but listen, / And accrue what I hear into myself . . . . and let sounds contribute toward me." Walt Whitman.

#2

A BRIEF HISTORY OF SECRETS

Gordon Lonsdale. William Vassall. Bruno Pontecorvo. Julius Rosenberg. Ethel Rosenberg. Guy Burgess. Donald Maclean. Harold Philby. All famous spies. All whose lives ended in prison, exile, or execution. Nations *trade* secrets; it has always been, and will always be, a valuable form of *commerce* that strengthens ties between territories. But when individuals *betray* the secrets of a nation, for personal gain or in accordance with the personal belief in a higher cause—which, you may be surprised to know, happens more frequently than the former —a nation *loses* power, and a direct threat to national security ensues, which is often—as was the case during the Second World War when spies absconded with secrets about nuclear fission—a direct threat to the lives of individual people waking and walking in that territory. Louise Glück says in her essay "Against Sincerity," "the secrets we choose to betray lose power over us," and that is a certain, if somewhat ambiguous, truth. If the secret has been destructive to us, we most eagerly would like to see its demise. This is the theory behind the belief that the fewer secrets a man has, the happier he is, for he is less separated or divided. This is the theory behind intimate conversations between friends or lovers, and the theory behind centuries of private conversations with clergy, taken over in the early twentieth century by private conversations with the therapist, taken over in the late twentieth century by pharmaceutical conversations with cells, which is based on the premise that the "secret," that which divides, rests not in thoughts, actions, or events but in our very cells, and there is much truth in this, for what is a cell but a depository of highly individualized secrets? But there is another side to "the secrets we choose to betray lose power over us" and that is that, in relinquishing a secret, we may lose a very important power indeed, one that nourishes, protects, and defines us. We may lose our life. We may lose what little or great personal power we possess, lose our sense of self, lose the energy that drives our soul. What is your PIN? And if you look at most of the great narrative literature in all cultures, you will see the proposition endlessly played out: Samson loses his hair (long believed to be the depository of strength and spirit), Moses gets put in a basket and sets sail among the rushes (the birth of a hero always involves a secret), Oedipus loses his sight (but gains insight), Faust loses his soul (but gains knowledge), foundlings discover their secret origins, changelings discover their secret origins, couples are free to marry because they are *not* siblings after all, couples are *not* free to marry because they *are* siblings, there is a mad former wife in the attic, and somewhere in the middle of all this mad discovery of secrets resulting in curse or blessing, Jean-Jacques Rousseau writes his *Confessions*, which are posthumously published and forever after change the face of literature: what frankness! Someone has set out to reveal the whole truth about none other than himself, the unpleasant as well as the pleasant, and Goethe and Tolstoy and Proust and Gide and Joyce have nothing to worry about, for the standard has been set, Wordsworth sits up in bed and thinks, "Why don't I make myself the subject of my own poetry?" and the fascinating panorama of literature trots on, never really leaving its preoccupation with secrets, only modifying it to include, stylistically, the voice of the autobiographical real over the more symbolic life span.

The idea of a secret that will be revealed always results in one of two scenarios: death and destruction, or self-discovery and recovery beyond our wildest dreams of unification. And in the greatest of sagas, both at the same time.

The simplest possible definition of a secret is something that "is kept from knowledge or observation." Such as ... sex, which is, in its human form, kept from observation. Or ... the meaning of human existence, which is secluded from our knowledge. And since existence originates in the sexual act, the two are forever linked in the minds of a self-conscious species.

The words *secret* and *sacred* are siblings.

The simplest possible definition of *sacred* is something so especially esteemed it is *set apart*, and consecrated as such. And by setting something apart one ensures against encroachment. Yet, despite this assurance, one sometimes lives in fear: the sacred word is a secret and cannot be spoken without consequence, be it blessing or curse. There is simply too much power in certain words, and the unnerving force of naming casts a great spell over language and, in one very important sense, created poetry, since to invoke sacred powers, bypass words were employed, incantations without any meaning at all, such as *abracadabra*, words that of course became imbued with as much power as what they were trying to invoke. And then, as often happens, it worked in reverse, so that very sacred words or phrases *bypassed themselves*, through a living version of the parlor game Password (sometimes called Gossip or Telephone), where a word is passed or repeated from ear to ear until it changes into gibberish. To my mind, the most paralyzing example of this process is one origin theory of the term *hocus-pocus*, that it was once *hoc est corpus*—*This is my body*—which Hugh Kenner calls "the most efficacious words in Christendom, the very words of consecration itself," the words spoken by the high priest at the high noon of the Roman Mass, when the metaphor becomes the thing itself.

The origins of poetry are clearly rooted in obscurity, in secretiveness, in incantation, in spells that must at once invoke and protect, tell the secret and keep it.

#3

"But why do you do all this reading? You are not a student any more."

"He would not read if he was," said the Mandelsloh. "Students do not read, they drink."

"Why do they drink?" Sophie asked.

"Because they desire to know the whole truth," said Fritz, "and that makes them desperate.". . .

"What would it cost them," Sophie asked, "to know the whole truth?"

"They can't reckon that," said Fritz, "but they know they can get drunk for three groschen."

PENELOPE FITZGERALD, *The Blue Flower*

4

Fragments are the husk of a secret.

Openmouthed, closemouthed.
Telling a secret and keeping a secret.

Emily Dickinson wrote 1,775 secrets, on tiny pieces of white paper, many of which were folded into notes, the kind you used to pass in high school. The kind of notes lovers in the Imperial Court of tenth-century Japan—which constituted a city—exchanged, using messengers, and Emily often did exactly what they did: attached flowers to the outside of the note, flowers representative of the season, or of the sentiments folded within. Great attention was paid to the concept of the whole note, from its outer wrappings to the time of day it was delivered, and when one went out—say as condolence to a neighbor who had lost a family member—imagine the sense of decorum and form on the *outside*; and at the core—those fragments! It must have been like a butterfly delivering its own empty cocoon.

It takes great courage to speak in fragments.
It takes great courage to speak in whole sentences.

Was spring a secret that winter carried? Of course it was. Spring now carries the secret of winter.

There is a case to be made for the traitor.

Anger is an emotion that is produced by fear. There are no exceptions. Fear is produced by loss, or the threat of loss, imagined or real. The loss of a secret makes one angry—if one's intent is to remain isolate. The loss of a secret makes one joyous, if one's intent is toward fellowship. Openmouthed, closemouthed. All secrets have an inside and an outside, they *must*, because they are concealed or hidden—that is their *nature*—and every secret is the perfect example of form and theory. Form *is* theory. The smallest, most portable, and perfect example of the form and theory of a secret is the fortune cookie. Our fortune, our future, is always unrevealed, thus concealed, thus a secret, thus the slip of paper is deposited *inside* the slip of dough. Imagine a fortune cookie with the fortune printed on the *outside* and you are imagining the failure to con*form* to theory. Whereas the small colored hearts that are an American commodity on Valentine's Day have their text—Call Me, Be Mine, Hot Stuff—written on the *outside*, because the theory of Valentine's Day is *expression*, the secret is out—interesting, though, is that we circulate the latter only once a year, while the former—the fortune cookie—is always with us. Richard Howard, in an open address, criticized the establishment of National Poetry Month as a betrayal of "the best-kept secret of all"—poetry. Every April, since the establishment of National

Poetry Month, I receive a call from my local library or high school, asking if I will participate in a reading. How about November? I always ask, and the answer is always the same: People aren't interested then; April is the month poetry goes public.

April is the cruelest month.
The secret of poetry is cruelty.

In order for a poem to speak, the mouth of the poem—the language—must open and close; the words of a poem must be steamed open like a clam, then shut down like a clam, and in doing so simulate real lips. Practice saying aloud the words *secret love*: feel how your mouth enacts the paradox implied by that phrase. To say the word *secret* one has to inhale—a repression of air—and to say the word *love* one has to exhale—an expression of air. Your tongue will have to retreat into the fortune cookie of your mouth and then semi-slip out on the revelatory word *love*. The linguistic tension of these two words, spoken together, perfectly embodies the joy and anguish of that sweet man, John Clare, who used them at the end of his great poem "I Hid My Love."

> I hid my love when young till I
> Couldn't bear the buzzing of a fly;

I hid my love to my despite
Till I could not bear to look at light:
I dare not gaze upon her face
But left her memory in each place;
Where'er I saw a wild flower lie
I kissed and bade my love good-bye.

I met her in the greenest dells,
Where dewdrops pearl the wood bluebells;
The lost breeze kissed her bright blue eye,
The bee kissed and went singing by,
A sunbeam found a passage there,
A gold chain round her neck so fair;
As secret as the wild bee's song
She lay there all the summer long.

I hid my love in field and town
Till e'en the breeze would knock me down;
The bees seemed singing ballads o'er,
The fly's bass turned a lion's roar;
And even silence found a tongue,
To haunt me all the summer long;
The riddle nature could not prove
Was nothing else but secret love.

Poems are written in secret. The writing of literature most often takes place in private, and serious as it is, it always has the aura of *play*, not work, because of its nonutilitarian nature. And Western culture has always fundamentally limited play, if not prohibited it, because of this nonutilitarian nature: it furthers nothing, just as the erotic act of sex, if engaged in for anything other than procreation, has a long history of religious prohibition (though religion in its origins, of course, did no such thing—I do not have the time to trace the history of religion in the West; you will have to trust me when I tell you that erotic prohibition played no part in its beginning). Poetry and sex have this in common: they are the instant consumption of energy, that is, they do not accumulate, they do not have a value *dependent* upon the consequences of furthering anything outside themselves, though of course they *can* do that, whereas religious morality is always dependent on consequence. Georges Bataille:

> If we do it in secret the prohibition transfigures what it prohibits and illumines it with a glow, at once sinister and divine: in a word, it illumines it with a religious glow. . . . Prohibition gives to what it proscribes a meaning that in itself the prohibited act never had.

Thus the act becomes sacred. And

> a sacred value remains nonetheless in its very principle an immediate value: it has meaning only in the instant of this transfiguration, wherein we pass [instantly] from use value

[zero] to ultimate value [100], a value independent from any
effect beyond the instant itself, and which is fundamentally
an aesthetic value.

Elsewhere Bataille says, "Eroticism cannot be entirely revealed
without poetry."

5

Victoria's *Secret* is, presumably, her crotch. In one of that
store's advertising posters, the only place where the crotch is
shown is at the center, that is, the crotch, of the picture and the
entire photograph is arranged to take the eye *away* from the
crotch as quickly as possible—her hand is directed upward and
the eye follows it, and the black glove of the other hand, on the
side of her thigh, moves the eye downward and to the side. But
with all the other models, whose crotches are *hidden*, the pho-
tography is arranged—I mean the position of the model's
hands, gloves, legs—so that our eye is directed *toward* what is
hidden—that is, the crotch. If you happen to see the picture,
check out the gloves, the knees, and the crossed hands of the
models. When the secret is exposed we look away. When the
secret is hidden we try to see it. That's really all I want to say
about this picture, although one could say many other things,
such as observing that these women appear to be men, as their

hats and gloves imply the appearance of an English gentleman, so the models might be saying something like, "You think we are women but we are men," that is, strong, assertive, aggressive, though, of course, they could be—and are—also saying, "You think we are men (by our outermost garments) but you see, once we take off our clothes we are women, here is the thin and delicate lace beneath the black hat." In fact, the only two words on the catalogue cover chosen especially for the photograph say much the same thing: *English Lace*. Stiff upper lip, reserve, dignity, the commerce of carrying on; something one can *see through*, like lace, that beautiful and vulnerable substance that for centuries was produced by hand at the cost of infinite pain: lace makers bleed and go blind in the production of veils.

6

Count Schimmelmann was sunk in contemplation of the Hyena, when the proprietor of the Menagerie came and addressed him. . . .

"Your Excellency does well to look at the Hyena," said he. "It is a great thing to have got a Hyena to Hamburg, where there has never been one till now. All Hyenas, you will know, are hermaphrodites, and in Africa, where they come from, on a full-moon night they will meet and join in a ring of copulation wherein each individual takes the double part of male and female. Did you know that?"

"No," said Count Schimmelmann, with a slight movement of disgust.

"Do you consider now, Your Excellency," said the showman, "that it should be, on account of this fact, harder to a Hyena than to other animals to be shut up by itself in a cage? Would he feel a double want, or is he, because he unites in himself the complementary qualities of creation, satisfied in himself, and in harmony? In other words, since we are all prisoners in life, are we happier, or more miserable, the more talents we possess?"

ISAK DINESEN, *Out of Africa*

7

The human mind hides from itself.

Or, Heraclitus, fragment 123: "being inclines intrinsically to self-concealment."

And this is not so far from what an astronomer said: Sometimes you get the feeling the universe is trying to prevent us from discovering the truth.

Sad fate! To be intrinsically inclined toward secrets!

Poetry is NEVER encoded—it is NEVER a covert operation whose information is ciphered and must be deciphered—and yet it does incline toward self-concealment, insofar as it concentrates intently on what words *conceal*, or, to put it another way, on what language seeks to *reveal*.

It concentrates on the inside in an attempt to reverse the situation; to turn it inside out.

Every word carries a secret inside itself; it's called *etymology*.

It is the DNA of a word. To crack or press a word is to use its etymology to reveal its secrets, all still embedded in the direct action of ancient and original metaphor. A poet may or may not know the etymology of his words—that seems to be a habit of temperament, or of classical training in Greek and Latin—but I have observed that very often a poet *unconsciously* intuits the etymology of a word while writing; sometimes we use a word whose meaning we do not know, but it sounds right, and when we look it up in the dictionary we are astonished to find its meaning fits beyond our wildest expectation, and sometimes we know the meaning of a word but some compulsion makes us look it up anyway and again we are astonished, for the secondary and tertiary meanings of the word are even better suited to our context than the one we knew—and so we go, until the word has released both its ancestry and its secret longing to be exactly what it is and where it is at that moment.

Cecilia Vicuña: "Words have a love for each other, a desire that culminates in poetry."

The subconscious—always a secret!—is made conscious. Words love each other! And the rise of consciousness is always a birth.

Carl Jung preferred the term *psychic energy* to *libido*, which he did not believe was exclusively sexual; he believed sexuality was only one of its many manifestations.

The psychic energy required and used in writing a poem is also a secret. Where did it come from? How did it get here and where is it going?

These are the questions we ask ourselves when we write, and these are the questions an astronomer asks of the stars.

Consider the word *consider*, which originally meant "to observe the stars."

Consideration leads to *comprehension*, which originally meant "to grasp, to seize something with the hands and hold it tight in the arms": what the mother does with the child. To hold, to put one's arms around.

As Jung once wittily noted: "When the neurotic complains that the world does not understand him, he is telling us in a word that he wants his mother."

And who among us is not neurotic, and has never complained that they are not understood? Why did you come here, to this place, if not in the hope of being *understood*, of being in some small way comprehended by your peers, and embraced by them in a fellowship of shared secrets?

I don't know about you, but I just want to be held.

To say that consideration leads to comprehension is to say that observation leads to action. The tasks of the outside world must be observed and then embraced privately, just as the astronomer looks through his telescope, considers the stars, and embraces the universe in the closed space of his mind.

Enter the cold dark matter.

Enter the anti-secret of every word. There is no comprehension. Our comprehension is limited. Language can only hold for a moment before the embrace disintegrates.

Whitman, the windbag, knew this, and opted for silence the night he walked out of the learned astronomer's lecture.

Then went home and wrote a poem about both.

Edmond Jabès, in some dark Parisian hole: "When you write you do not know whether you are obeying the moment or eternity."

And Tomas Tranströmer when he cried in the Nordic night: "So much that can neither be written nor kept inside!"

A poet may know that the most eloquent word is a stone, but he must never say that or the silence would be broken, the silence he keeps by speaking—

The word *paradox* is a literary cliché, we use it and say it so lightly. It is a kind of fabric softener. "The conscious mind . . . is not always either willing or able to put forth the extraordinary intellectual and moral effort needed to take a paradox seriously." Jung.

The two sides of a secret are repression and expression, just as the two sides of the poem are the told and the untold. We must be careful not to take the word as the meaning itself; words do not "capture" a moment as much as they "communicate" it—they are a bridge that, paradoxically, breaks isolation and loneliness without eradicating it. It is the first experience you ever had of reading a decent poem: "Oh, somebody else is lonely, too!"

It is the most fragile relationship in the world.

Colette calls a poem "that secret, that dried rose, that scar, that sin." James Tate uses as an epigraph for one of his books a line by James Salter: "Here then, faintly discolored and liable to come apart if you touch it, is the corsage that I kept from the dance."

In Hindu poetics, "a poem is recognized as such by those who have a heart." If you do not have a heart, you cannot recognize a poem.

The heart is a small closed space, a symbol or souvenir of the inner life, the secret life, the silent life.

It is liable to come apart if you touch it.

André Gide: "Suffering consists in being unable to reveal one-self and, when one happens to succeed in doing so, in having nothing more to say." Such is the life cycle of a secret: some-thing is repressed, then expressed, leaving a void that fills again with repressions.

Tranströmer, in his long poem "Baltics," writes this:

> Sometimes you wake up at night
> and quickly throw some words down
> on the nearest paper, on the margin of a newspaper
> (the words glowing with meaning!)
> but in the morning: the same words don't say anything
> anymore, scrawls, misspeakings.

Often when I read poetry my experience of it is so intense, so complete and whole, yet afterward it is as if I am defeated; I am unable to remember, I am unable to bring back into my life what I have been listening to, just as all living beings—literacy is of no consequence here—have in their lives moments of be-ing but later lose them, no less than the poet who has broken his pencil, or woken up. Infuriating as this is, we need to re-mind ourselves of something once put like this:

> To raise the question of the mind is to call everything into
> question; all is disorder. . . . But this disorder is the condi-

tion and promise of the mind's fecundity, which depends on the unexpected rather than the expected, on what we do not know (and because we do not know it) rather than on what we know.

PAUL VALÉRY

If we do not forget, what is there to remember?

When we sit down to write, The Comforter, The Mind's Promise, The Beautiful Order of Thistles, has gone away and hidden, but if it go not away and hide, how can it come to us?

I do not really see, at this point in my life, any difference between repression and expression.

Though, on the surface, as an *expression*, it seems as if an idiot is speaking.

People, the people we really love, where did they come from? What did we do to deserve them?

8

For a long time I wanted a tattoo.

I knew exactly what I wanted and where I wanted it. I wanted a small door, neither closed nor open. I wanted a small door slightly ajar. I had forgotten this, or half-forgotten it, when I read *The Poetics of Space*, where Gaston Bachelard devotes two pages to the image of a half-open door—"On May nights, when so many doors are closed, there is one that is barely ajar"—and concludes that "man is half-open being."

I was confused about the words *immanent* and *imminent*. So I looked them up. They are spelled differently. One means "existing inherently, remaining within always." The other means "about to happen."

When you are walking down a city street and not paying much attention—perhaps you are downtrodden by some confusion—and come suddenly upon a rosebush blooming against a brick wall, you may be struck and awakened by the appearance of beauty. But the rose is not beautiful. You think the rose is beautiful and so you may also think, with sadness, that it will die. But the rose is not beauty. What beauty is is your ability to apprehend it. The ability to apprehend beauty *is* the human spirit and it is what all such moments are about, which is why such moments occur in places and at times that may strike another as unlikely or inconceivable, and it does not seem far-fetched to say that the larger the human spirit, the more it will apprehend beauty in increasingly unlikely and inconceivable situations, which is why there is such a great variety of art objects on earth. And there is something else we should say about the apprehension of beauty: it causes *discomfort*; and by discomfort I mean the state of being *riled*, which is a state of *reverberation*.

What you carried inside you when you walked through the door was this ability. It is your ability to apprehend beauty, or the lack of it. It is your ability to listen. And change, or be changed. It has something to do with the secret of human existence, which is nowhere revealed, and nowhere concealed, and in front of which we remain, or become, infants.

Mallarmé in a letter dated July 16, 1866:

> Every man has a secret in him, many die without finding it, and will never find it because they are dead, it no longer exists, nor do they. I am dead and risen again with the jeweled key of my last spiritual casket. It is up to me now to open it in the absence of any borrowed impression, and its mystery will emanate in a sky of great beauty.

We speak of secrets from the point of view of the teller or keeper, but what of the listener? What about the one who *hears* the secret? What happens to him?

The listener is made *uncomfortable*. The bearer of the secret may be unburdened, but the *hearer* is now burdened. This is the heartbeat of all exchange. It goes by many names, and one that is not perhaps chiefest among them, but is nonetheless important to us, is *reading*.

> The barriers of personality fall, the joys and sorrows of humanity accumulate within oneself and the individual pours himself into the collectivity and unreservedly experiences whatever is allotted to humanity.
>
> HELLMUT WILHELM

An expansion takes place, the hearer is made to feel human, alive; he feels as though the teller's being were his own, and so experiences a change of being where that which is *inside* himself takes on the proportions of that which is *outside* himself.

It is the listener who is then silent.
For he is the bearer of the secret now.

The whole world seems to be growing inside him.

What is the source of our first suffering? It lies in the fact that we hesitated to speak. . . . It was born in the moments when we accumulated silent things within us.

BACHELARD, *Water and Dreams*

9

In the end I would rather wonder than know.
I never got my tattoo, and never will.
I hesitated too long, and the time in which one acquires such things passed, as all things will.

Because I would rather wonder than know, my interests and talents lie in the arts rather than the sciences, although, like the monk who discovered champagne—an accidental event that unexpectedly happened to his wine—I have on occasion come running with open arms toward another with the news, "Look! I am drinking the stars!"

#10

I spake openly to the world; . . . and in secret have I said
nothing. Why askest thou me? Ask them which heard me,
what I have said unto them: behold, they know what I said.

Those words are attributed to Christ in the Gospel according
to John. And since it is always good to let God have the last
word, let us end by repeating them.

I spake openly to the world; . . . and in secret have I said
nothing. Why askest thou me? Ask them which heard me,
what I have said unto them: behold, they know what I said.

ON FEAR

I suppose, as a poet, among my fears can be counted the deep-seated uneasiness surrounding the possibility that one day it will be revealed that I consecrated my life to an imbecility. Part of what I mean—what I *think* I mean—by "imbecility" is *something intrinsically unnecessary and superfluous* and thereby unintentionally cruel. It was a Master who advised that we speak little, better still say nothing, unless we are quite sure that what we wish to say is true, kind, and helpful. But how can a poet, whose role is to *speak*, adhere to this advice? How can anyone whose role is to facilitate language speak little or say nothing? I don't know if other poets have this fear, but if they do not, I reason it will only increase the anguish of the outcome if it one day passes into being. *To pass into being*—now there's a fear no one ever had. No one ever feared being born, even when all those responsible for the event were fraught with fear for the unborn. And if I may segue to a child at the age of four, I recall watching a four-year-old girl being approached by a dog that was, well, much *larger* than the girl herself. The girl's face was astonishing to watch. It was completely elastic and changed from an expression of wonder and glee: *Please come to me doggie and we shall play oh what happiness to be approached by you*—to—in less than ten seconds—an expression of sheer terror: *Fear! fear! doggie will eat me up and mommie is far away*. As the dog slowly crossed the room, in what could not have been more than two minutes, the girl's face changed expressions so many times I gave up counting. As she oscillated between feeling secure and insecure, it struck me that her face would probably continue to change, albeit at a slower rate, every time she was approached by a dog for the next couple of years, one day coming to rest on that expression that was likely to signify forever after how this human being felt about dogs. But something seemed to be missing from my neat little formula; surely the dog's face was important, too? This dog was eager and friendly, if a bit clumsy, but what if the next dog took a good-sized chunk out of the child's face? I asked the poet Tony Hoagland what he thought about fear. He said fear was the *ghost* of an experience: we fear the reoccurrence of a pain we once felt, and in this way fear is like a hangover. The memory of our pain is a pain unto itself, and thus feeds our fear like a foyer with mirrors on both sides. And then he quoted Auden: "And ghosts must do again / What gives them pain." It is interesting to note that this idea—fear's being the ghost of pain, or imaginary pain—figures in psychological torture by the CIA;

in fact, their experiments with pain found that imaginary pain was more effective than physical pain—poets, take note—and thus psychological torture more effective than physical torture. Here is an excerpt from their *Exploitation Training Manual*, written in 1983: "The threat of coercion usually weakens or destroys resistance more effectively than coercion itself. For example, the threat to inflict pain can trigger fears more damaging than the immediate sensation of pain." Although I have never been bitten by a dog, I am scared to death of them, as I am of all living creatures, including myself and my own fragmentation in the long hall of mirrors. James Ward, future British psychologist, broke with religion as a young man in 1872, but found himself a bundle of reflexes over which he had no choice and no control. He said: "I have no dread of God, no fear of the Devil, no fear of man, but my head swims as I write it—*I fear myself*." What do I mean by fear? Why I mean that thing that drives you to write, but let us step out of the foyer, and back onto the street, back down the road, and make our approach somewhat more slowly. Sometime after I had already written the pages you are about to sit through, I realized I had been using the wrong word throughout. *Dread* is a more accurate version of what I am thinking about, and I have Julian of Norwich, a fifteenth-century anchorite, to thank for pointing this out. In her *Revelations of Divine Love*, the account of a vision she had during an illness in her thirty-first year, she says, "I believe dread can take four forms." In a nutshell, the first of these forms is what I will describe as the unconscious *emotion* fear—your very first response to the smell of smoke, the sound of thunder, the sight of flames, the slap. The second form of dread is the anticipatory dread of pain, either physical, emotional, spiritual, or psychological, and that, folks, covers nine-tenths of the world's surface. The third form of dread is doubt, or despair. And the fourth form of dread is "born of reverence," the holy dread with which we face that which we love most, or that which loves us the most. *Dread.* I like it better than the word *fear* because fear, like the unconscious emotion which is one of its forms, has only the word *ear* inside of it, telling an animal to listen, while dread has the word *read* inside of it, telling us to read carefully and find the *dead*, who are also there. But I have not used the word *dread* in what follows. I have used the word *fear*. And *fear* is an older word—it can be found in Old English, while *dread* enters the language in Middle English. Neurobiologists have distinguished emotions from feelings, though I am afraid our language has for so long used the two terms as equivalent currency that it is a hopeless task to expect any listener to hear one word and not think of the other. Emotions are hardwired, biological functions of the nervous system such as fear, terror, sexual attraction, and hunger-impelled action (also called "feeding behaviors"). They are each purely physical reactions over which one has no control, and they are common to all animals with a central nervous system. The emotion of fear is what drives all animals away from life-threatening situations, and that is not the kind of fear I have in mind. Feelings, on the other hand, are more complicated and involve cognitive reactions that combine, or can be combined, with emotions, memories, experience, and *intelligence*. That is the kind of fear I have in mind—the feeling of fear that involves an intelligent, cognitive reaction. Fear that requires self-consciousness. Don't be alarmed, scientists are not studying *feelings*, they are only studying emotions, divorced from cognition, as they travel in recognizable systems throughout the brain and the body. At this juncture it might be instructive of me to look up at you and say, "Try putting less emotion, and more feeling, into your poems." The fact that neurobiologists have publicly announced the separation of emotion from feeling should be heartening news to poets everywhere, for it implies that to have feelings is on par with highly sophisticated cognitive systems. Feelings are not subpar. On the other hand, lest we forget, let me repeat: to be more emotional and less cognitive is to be less evolved than the species is able to be. It is to be like a four-year-old child. Feelings seem to represent a place where emotions *combine* with intelligence and experience to create a highly personal thought process that results in an individual's worldview. And that is where I want to take up our fear again. I asked a doctor about fear. The doctor said, "The only way to overcome fear is to do what you are trained to do. Fear is overcome by procedure. For example, if I don't successfully insert an emergency trach—a hole in the throat—someone will die from lack of oxygen. So I mechanically do what I have been trained to do. Someone is there, periodically calling out the oxygen saturation—95, 90, 88, 83, 79—and the lower it gets the more of an emergency it becomes. And the funny thing is, I ask for the count. It is part of the procedure, but I work as if I am not listening—procedural concentration is all."

I asked a pilot about fear. The pilot said, "The only way to overcome fear is to do what you are trained to do. Fear is overcome by procedure. For example, I was flying a test jet alone at 30,000 feet and there was a leak in my oxygen mask I didn't know about. I temporarily lost consciousness, and when I came to I was at 15,000 feet heading straight for the ground, nose down, completely out of control—and I was still groggy, still fighting for consciousness. Cut the throttle and punch the dive brakes. Cut the throttle and punch the dive brakes. Cut the throttle and punch the dive brakes. Those were the only thoughts I had, and I continued to have them until I leveled out at 5,000 feet." Then the doctor and the pilot, who were in the same room with me, looked at me and said, "So, have you ever had any poetry emergencies?" I was a fool on a fool's errand. Out of the fear of being a fool, I wanted to tell them that the fear they were trained to overcome was an emotion and not a feeling; after all, these were both life-threatening situations and their reactions were pure instinct, albeit professional ones. But I have professional instincts as well, professional instincts I employ while writing a poem. I was hopelessly confused and felt my sense of self-worth losing altitude; in situations like this I pick up the phone and call my friend, the German philosopher. "Reinhard," I shouted into the phone, "What do you think about fear?" "Yikes!" he shouted back, "I am afraid of dogs." At last, a friend. And then he quoted Nietzsche: "The degree of fearfulness is the measure of intelligence." It was better than I had hoped. Cut the throttle and punch the dive brakes. "Fear is to recognize ourselves." As far back as I could remember, every minute of my life had been an emergency in which I was paralyzed with fear. Feelings of fear, being at least in part cognitive, and therefore thoughts, often constitute knowledge. For instance, the knowledge that one is going to die. This is a fear one can have while lying in a hammock on a beautiful day. And it can lead to an emergency of feeling that often results in a poem. "Thank you," I said, before hanging up, and then I heard my friend Reinhard say, "Faulkner, however, said that for a writer, the basest of all things is to be afraid." My mind quickly came to the conclusion Faulkner was drunk at the time. But perhaps he was thinking about writer's block, the inability of a writer to do that which is most natural to him: to encounter fear, to face fear; a fear of being alone with fear . . .

Roethke: "Fear was my father, Father fear. / His look drained the stones."

Auden: "Fear gave his watch no look."

Neruda: "When I was a young poet I was full of fear like a real rat in a corner."

And what are we to make of Wordsworth, "Fostered alike by beauty and by fear"?

Or Milton's "equal poise of hope and fear"? Or Blake's "fearful symmetry"?

Which is more inexpressible, the beautiful or the terrifying? Gerard Manley Hopkins, in his last, troubled sonnets, cries out, "O which one? is it each one?" Lorca says, "The poet who embarks on the creation of a poem (experience has shown) begins with the aimless sensation of a hunter about to embark on a night hunt through the remotest of forests. Unaccountable dread stirs in his heart." And Edmond Jabès, in *The Book of Questions*: "*If you bend over your page . . . and do not suddenly tremble with fear, throw away your pen. Your writing would have little value.*"

And George Oppen, who said, "Great artists are those who, in the end, do not have a failure of nerve." Afraid, yes, but there they are, having locked themselves alone in a room with fear. Or as someone else might put it: "Blank pages—shoot-out at the O.K. Corral."

I think it is time to list some concrete fears:

> fear of death
> of illness
> of pain
> of suffering
> of despair

of not understanding
of disturbance or reversal of powers
of being unloved
of the unknown or strange
of destruction
of humiliation
of degradation
of poverty
of hunger
of aging
of unworthiness
of transgression
of punishment
of making a mistake
of loss of dignity
of failure
of oblivion
of outliving the mind
of eating an anchovy.

These are not simian fears. These are human fears.

Barry Lopez, in his study of the Arctic called *Arctic Dreams*, makes this interesting observation:

Eskimos do not maintain this intimacy with nature without paying a certain price. When I have thought about the ways in which they differ from people in my own culture, I have realized that they are more afraid than we are. On a day-to-day basis, they have more fear. Not of being dumped into cold water from an umiak, not a debilitating fear. They are afraid because they accept fully what is violent and tragic in nature. It is a fear tied to their knowledge that sudden, cataclysmic events are as much a part of life, of really living, as are the moments when one pauses to look at something beautiful. A Central Eskimo shaman named Aua, queried by Knud Rasmussen about Eskimo beliefs, answered, "We do not believe. We fear."

Lopez goes on to chastise those who think hunting peoples such as the Eskimos are living in perfect harmony with nature. Nervous awe and apprehension are born out of proximity and attention. The greater the intimacy between these cultures and nature, the greater the tension. The industrial world destroys nature not because it doesn't love it but because it is not afraid of it. You can in your own minds recall the long Judeo-Christian tradition of fearing God. Or you can perhaps remember having read *The Wind in the Willows* as a child, or to a child, and encountering that magnificent, odd, and out-of-place chapter entitled "The Piper at the Gates of Dawn" where Mole and Rat go in search of Otter's lost son and find, on the very edge of dawn, Nature personified in the august presence of a terrifying and benevolent satyr, half man, half animal:

"Rat!" he found breath to whisper, shaking. "Are you afraid?"

"Afraid?" murmured the Rat, his eyes shining with un-utterable love. "Afraid? Of *Him*? O, never, never! And yet—and yet—O, Mole, I am afraid!"

Then the two animals, crouching to the earth, bowed their heads and did worship.

Fear is the greatest motivator of all time. Conflict born of fear is behind our every action, driving us forward like the cogs of a clock. Fear is desire's dark dress, its doppelgänger. "Love and dread are brothers," says Julian of Norwich. As desire is wanting and fear is not-wanting, they become inexorably linked; just as desire can be destructive (the desire for power), fear can be constructive (fear of hurting another); fear of poverty becomes desire for wealth. Collective actions are not exempt from these double powers; consider this succinct and frightening sentence written by John Berger:

> Everywhere these days more and more people knock their heads against the fact that the future of our planet and what it will offer or deny to its inhabitants, is being decided by boards of men who control more money than all of the governments in the world, who never stand for election, and whose sole criterion for every decision they take is whether or not it increases or is prone to increase Profit.

But has it ever been any different? Races everywhere have always been at the mercy of collective desire and collective fear, sometimes their own, sometimes others'.

The impulse toward order is born of fear and desire, and the impulse toward chaos is born of the same. The British psychoanalyst D. W. Winnicott believed artists were people driven by the tension between the desire to communicate and the desire to hide.

Think of the simplest caricature of a poet, the kind that might be used as a generic figure in a cartoon. Which comes to mind, the forlorn, melancholy, sadly loitering one, suicidal in blue breeches, or the happy eater and drinker, the smeller of roses, the carouser, the gusto-bearing, sun-loving one? In Epicurean atomic theory, "the world functions because from the outset there is a lack of balance." The French novelist Georges Perec, devoted to mathematical literary forms—he wrote a novel without the letter *e* in it—speaks of anti-constraints within a system of restraints. He quotes the painter Paul Klee: "Genius is 'an error in the system.'" (Those of you who have heard lectures on the sonnet may recall that this is often, precisely, the point.) The world functions because of fear, because of the error, the anti-constraint, the anti-perfect, the anti-balance. We stumble. We fall.

We fail. And so desire to progress, to become better poets, to eradicate a disease, to become better people, to perfect that which is perpetually imperfect. The biblical "fall" is just such an anti-constraint. The apple was fear. (And remember, fear is knowledge, according to Nietzsche.) The apple set the world in motion by forcing Adam and Eve to migrate out of the Perfect. "Fear is to recognize ourselves," said the philosopher. One of the fears a young writer has is not being able to write as well as he or she wants to, the fear of not being able to sound like X or Y, a favorite author. But out of fear, hopefully, is born a young writer's voice: "But now," says Kierkegaard, "to strive to become what one already is: who would take the pains to waste his time on such a task, involving the greatest imaginable degree of resignation? . . . But for this very reason alone it is a very difficult task, . . . precisely because every human being has a strong natural bent and passion to become something more and different." It is very easy to read those words, and very hard to enact them. Elsewhere Kierkegaard says, "What is education? I should suppose that education was the curriculum one had to run through in order to catch up with oneself."

There are poets who are resigned to not being able to save the world, who barely have enough time to catch up with themselves and the attendant mystery of their fear and being. I suppose Szymborska is one of them. Here is her compatriot Miłosz describing her:

> In Szymborska we are divided not into the flesh and a surviving oeuvre [as in the tradition in Western literature running parallel to the Christian conception of immortality

through posterity] but into 'the flesh and a broken whisper'; poetry is no more than a broken whisper, quickly dying laughter. . . .

When it is not the perfection of a work that is important but expression itself, 'a broken whisper,' everything becomes, as it has been called, écriture. . . . To talk about anything, just to talk, becomes an operation in itself, a means of assuaging fear.

Much as I am sympathetic to the theory of *écriture*, I find it —confusing. For why is it meaningless to write with no other function than to assuage fear? Doesn't that function in itself have a meaning? And why fear the dismantling of language's semantic function, its being representational of meaning, when that is but one more *fear* that will drive those in opposition to *écriture* to write? And certainly this "theory" is no theory at all but a centuries-old practice: "He seemed to be depressed, for he went on writing" reads a twelfth-century Japanese text. Or take Rilke: "I have taken action against fear. I sat up the whole night and wrote; and now I am as thoroughly tired as after a long walk in the fields at Ulsgaard." Even a bitter poem is a small act of affirmation, and I wonder if we can't say the same thing about a meaningless poem (if such a thing exists). But Miłosz, who would most certainly disagree, is, to his immortal credit, a knight of faith, and I am but a knight of resignation. Like Kierkegaard: "As far as I am concerned, I am able to describe most excellently the movements of faith; but I cannot make them myself." The Danish philosopher's famous essay *Fear and Trembling* is a rumination on the biblical story of Abraham and Isaac. God asked Abraham to kill Isaac, Abraham's long-awaited and cherished son, and in the essay Kierkegaard grapples with how an act of murder can become a pleasing, good, and holy act in the eyes of God. It takes faith, a faith Kierkegaard minutely examines and describes, but one that he cannot in the end claim for himself, as devout as he is. He remains what he dubs a knight of resignation, a state that, for all it is worth, is still a state of sin. To be sure, I am "using" Miłosz here for my own purposes. He knows perfectly well he is not a saint. In an interview he has stated—and proved—that he is a man of contradiction. In other words, an ordinary man. But I admire his insistence on an objective reality, his faith in a world and an order that does not exist exclusively in the mind. And he is quite provocative at the end of his essay "Sand in the Hourglass":

If in our moments of happiness, mastery, ecstasy, we say Yes to heaven and to earth, and all we need is misfortune, sickness, the decline of physical powers to start screaming No, this means that all our judgments can be refuted tomorrow and that it is easy to mistake our life for the world. It is not obvious, however, why weakness—whether of a particular person or of an entire historical era—should be privileged and why the old nihilist from Beckett's *Krapp's Last Tape* should be closer to the truth than he himself was when he was twenty years old.

[In Beckett's play, an old man listens to tapes of himself speaking in his youth while responding with guttural sounds.]

Miłosz closes his essay with an astonishing and succinct remark of Simone Weil's: " 'I am suffering.' It is better to say this than to say, 'This landscape is ugly.' "

Fear belongs to man, not to the world. The world feels no fear, at any time, in any place. We are "an unhappy people in a happy world"—Wallace Stevens's last stance. Feelings of fear —personal, cognitive fear—allow us to feel anguish while lying in a hammock on a beautiful day, allow us to feel as if our life were threatened when the sky is blue and the meadow at peace. Raymond Queneau:

> The poet is never "inspired," if by inspiration we mean . . . a function of the poet's mood, the temperature, the political situation, subjective accidents, or the subconscious.
>
> The poet is never inspired because he is the master of what others assume to be inspiration. . . . He's never inspired because he's always inspired, because the powers of poetry are always at his disposal, obedient to his will, receptive to his guidance.

And I want to say the poet is never afraid because he is unceasingly afraid, and therefore cannot become that which he already is, though of course, Mr. Kierkegaard reminds us, he must; you might say fear *is* the poet's procedure, that which he has been trained to concentrate on. What an odd thing to say; what a terrible thing to say. Surely someone is saying to himself, "Gee whiz, hasn't she ever heard of *negative capability*?" As a matter of fact, I have; those words have become like a sickness unto death for me. As often as I have used them myself, I wish there were a moratorium on them for a quarter of a decade, so overused are they, so bandied about that they have come to mean just about anything one wants them to, especially a bebop version of Be Here Now, or a diffusive religious awe in which the poet wanders, forever in a stupor. As with most famous sayings, we are given only a fragment of the paragraph from which it comes. "*Negative capability*, that is, when man is capable of being in uncertainties, Mysteries, doubts, without any irritable reaching after fact & reason": the letter was written by John Keats on a Sunday, late in December of 1817, from Hampstead, and addressed to his brothers George and Tom. The year 1817 is, relatively speaking, quite early in Keats's career, though only four years before his death; the letter was written before George left for America, before Tom died, before John met Fanny Brawne, before he was sick, and before he had written what are considered his finest poems. One of the things you have to remember about Keats is that his development as a poet was telescoped into an intensely short period of time in which he passed through as many stages as another poet may experience in a life three times as long. Although the letter in its entirety is too long to quote here, you'll have to trust me when I say that only the last quarter of it puts his definition of negative capability into context. Here is that context:

> Several things dovetailed in my mind, & at once it struck me, what quality went to form a Man of Achievement especially in Literature & which Shakespeare possessed so enormously—I mean *Negative Capability*, that is when man is capable of being in uncertainties, Mysteries, doubts, without any irritable reaching after fact & reason—Coleridge, for instance, would let go by a fine isolated verisimilitude caught from the Penetralium of mystery, from being incapable of remaining content with half-knowledge. This pursued through Volumes would perhaps take us no further than this, that with a great poet the sense of Beauty overcomes every other consideration, or rather obliterates all consideration.

The passage is a bit like the United States Constitution. By that I mean that it may be interpreted to suit the purposes of a great many people who are at odds with one another. For instance, nothing prevents someone from saying that the essential definition means: once depressed, stay depressed. Of the passage relating to Coleridge there is no doubt: all you have to know is that Coleridge was the great intellectual among the Romantics, the great thinker. But an interesting and further complicating key is provided by the phrase "isolated verisimilitude." Verisimilitude means "having the *appearance* of a truth; probable," so that Keats is saying something like this: "Coleridge would pass over a probability that someone else would accept as the truth because Coleridge is not content with appearance or probability." If we add to this the idea of isolating, which implies distinction or differentiation, we can't help but think that Keats has *searched* the penetralium of mystery at least long enough to isolate a probable truth that is, unto him, sufficient. And this is a far cry from the nonisolating attitude that most of us associate with negative capability. Following this, Keats does a remarkable thing—he sums up something he has not even elaborated on. He says, "This pursued through volumes would perhaps take us no further than this, that with a great poet the sense of Beauty overcomes every other consideration, or rather obliterates all consideration." What does this mean? For where was there ever any mention of Beauty in the original definition? And do you see how this last bit could be used as a defense by the most archly formal poet or by his worst nemesis? And if I presume to understand negative capability, am I then incapable of it, since it *is* the capability of being in the presence of an uncertainty without reaching to understand it? And finally, we always intimately connect John Keats with negative capability as if he possessed it himself, as if he were speaking of himself, when he was not thinking or speaking of himself at all but of *Shakespeare*—and who among us amounts to squat compared to *Him*—of whom we can be as uncertain as we like without reaching after facts, because there are none? Shakespeare's reputation as a god is enhanced tenfold by the mysterious circumstances of his being. As is always the case, the unknown raises the stakes and the stature and the flag of the formidable before which we bow and do worship in unaccountable dread. Keats sought to understand much in his life; his poems and letters are full of urgent searching, of the kinds of questions that arise in the minds of passionate youth. He says in another letter: "You tell me never to despair—I wish it was as easy for me to observe the saying—truth is I have a horrid Morbidity of Temperament which has shown itself at intervals—it is I have no doubt the greatest Enemy and stumbling block I have to fear—I may even say that it is likely to be the cause of my disappointment." One has only to look at the opening lines of a majority of his poems to see him posited in a state of uncertainty, mystery, doubt—that is, fear:

"When I have fears that I may cease to be"
"Glory and loveliness have passed away"
"My spirit is too weak—mortality weights heavily on me"
"O thou whose face has felt the Winter's wind"
"In drear-nighted December"

"Deep in the shady sadness of a vale"
"If by dull rhymes our English must be chained"
"O what can ail thee, knight-at-arms"
"Why did I laugh tonight? . . ."
"My heart aches . . ."

The suffering in these poems remains intact; it is neither re-solved nor negated. What happens for the most part is, the po-ems *dissolve*, finally, into the cream of the physical world. If negative capability works at all, it works in reverse, a kind of negative Negative Capability—which would make it positive— where very real anxiety and irritability over mystery and doubt enables the poet—no, *propels* him—into the world of the eye, the pure perceptual habit that checks all cognitive drives, not before they've begun but *after* they've begun, and done their damage. In the words of a painter, the abstract expressionist Pat Adams: "That marveling rush of wonder at sheer multi-plicity and differentiation of stuff when surfaces of heightened materiality, of encrusted and layered imprinting are generated to entangle our attention and delay cognition"—until it seems that perpetual fear is a propellant into the innocent, fearless, and vulnerable world of the senses. So that the poet paralyzed with fear lying in a hammock on a beautiful day—unhappy man in a happy world—does not suffer any less when he looks around him; he does not cease to suffer, *he only ceases to try to understand.*

It was the last nostalgia: that he
Should understand. That he might suffer or that
He might die was the innocence of living, if life
Itself was innocent.

STEVENS, "Esthétique du Mal"

We do not know the etymology of the word *fear*. That is, the makers of dictionaries are unsure of it. But there is a good chance that it is related to the word *fare* in its oldest sense, which is to pass through, to go through, as in, *How did you fare at the dentist's?* or *Fare-thee-well*, or, He fared in this life like *one whose name was writ in water.*

Keats died at an age when no one should have to die. I wonder if the young are less afraid of dying, or more afraid of dying, than the old. I am no longer young. I am old enough *to understand and know* that it is not death I am afraid of, it's dying. Dying is the act, most often painful, that leads to death, while death itself is as painless as the feeling you had before you were born—no feeling at all, you didn't care one way or another (feeling is caring one way or another). *But what do I know?* Blessed Brother André, currently under investigation for sainthood, said, "If we knew the value of suffering, we would ask for it." Though others can, I cannot fathom that remark, let alone embrace it. Nor am I a Buddhist, one who believes suffering is based on ignorance, and that ignorance can be eradicated; actually, I *do* believe that suffering is based on ignorance (if the Third Reich had not been ignorant, millions would not have had to perish), but I don't believe ignorance can be eradicated. Actually, I *do* believe ignorance can be eradicated, but in the way of a weed—it will only pop up again someplace else. When Brother André asks us to embrace suffering, is he saying, "If we knew the value of ignorance, we would ask for it?" Should we finally and willingly cease to understand? I have often said I would rather wonder than know. Is that a youthful stance, a Keatsian stance? Is that—could it be—negative capability? Should one mature *beyond it*? I don't know. Rilke advises the young to "live the questions now," because the answers can only be revealed in time, the extension of which they do not possess. Much like Keats himself says, in a letter, that certain lessons can only be learned on the touchstone of the heart, that is, through direct experience.

What has life taught me? I am much less afraid than I ever was in my youth—of everything. That is a fact. At the same time, I feel more afraid than ever. And the two, I can assure you, are not opposed but inextricably linked. I am more or less the same age Emily Dickinson was when she died. Here is what she thought: "Had we the first intimation of the Definition of Life, the calmest of us would be Lunatics!" The calm lunatic—now that is something to aspire to.

MADNESS, RACK, AND HONEY

I don't know where to begin because I have nothing to say, yet I know that before long I will sound as if I'm on a crusade. What form does a lecture take when one has nothing to say? Let it take the form of a letter, an epistle, a form that gave rise, more than a thousand years after Alexander and Darius exchanged letters on the eve of a great battle, to the novel as we know it, at a time when the middle class was seeded and people began to believe that a life could be made or unmade, rise or fall, based on *gumption*, that opposite of fate, and that charting such a life might be of interest; a time when the postal business was also rising, with its own charts and systems and byways and roundabouts and rendezvousing on the highways (also new, not yet paved), and a belief that there might be, between ordinary men and women, conversation *at a distance*, and that one might learn how to read and how to write and put these skills to some use, maybe waste a little time while they were at it, and maybe come to see that the wasting of time is the most personal, most private, most intimate form of conversation with *oneself*, as well as another. Dear listener, you probably do not remember, because our paths had not yet crossed, that some years ago for a lecture, I collected newspaper and magazine ads that used the word *poetry* in them. I still do. My latest find was an ad for a Coach bag.

(Surely we must stop here and remind ourselves that letters first went by human courier, then by horse, next by *coach*, the letters weighting a large leather pouch, a well-oiled bag, impervious to raindrops, with a wide flap, not unlike the one my local rural route carrier carries and that I am sometimes lucky enough to catch a glimpse of in the backseat of her Jeep.) But back to the ad: a Coach bag is a luxury leather item. It is well-made and very, very expensive. This briefcase cost $412. I don't like the design of it, but that is another matter (or is it?). I love that it has that extra $12 tacked on to its price. That extra $12 is very *poetic*, by which I mean it is a particular detail that makes the price sound ever so real; it is much more believable than if the Coach company had said, simply, $400. The Coach company will suffer no fools; they know that the product they are trying to sell is based on details and its price should reflect those details in more ways than one. *In more ways than one.* Hmm, very poetic. Their latest ad campaign features the children, grandchildren, and great-grandchildren of famous people. I notice that these people are never photographed in settings of their own choosing, but are placed in settings that reflect and symbolize their illustrious ancestors. Emerson's great-granddaughter looking at a pond, Jesse Owens's granddaughter on a track, Gary Cooper's daughter showing some home movies. And here we have Albert Einstein's great-grandson sitting under a tree. Newton comes to mind. The young Mr. Einstein is dressed as a well-to-do Ivy League professor of the old school (his clothes and shoes are also by Coach, yet his great-grandfather was hopelessly sloppy). He is surrounded by more books than could possibly fit into his briefcase. They are "science" books, but not the kind of science books scientists read—there are old-fashioned high school textbooks in the foreground and what look like coffee-table science books— high-gloss gifts—and then some science books for laymen are scattered all around. There are three copies of a book called *Wisdom* in the picture, and our subject is reading one of them. What I like best of all in the picture are his eyes. Paul Einstein has his great-grandfather's eyes, and they are worth looking at. Yet of course his eyes belong to him, and they are saying, "I am feeling fairly ridiculous at this moment." Beyond that, I know very little about Paul Einstein. The fine-print copy for the ad says: "Paul Einstein is an accomplished violinist who enjoys reading literature, philosophy, and fine poetry." He's certainly no scientist, and probably hasn't read the book he's pictured reading. I don't know if he's a professional or amateur violinist and it is not clear what he does for a living, but he "enjoys reading literature, philosophy, and fine poetry." And I wonder who said that, Paul or the Coach copywriter? If I knew, I would know at least whom to address my questions to. Why the distinction *fine* poetry when no such distinction is used with literature or philosophy? Why do literature and philosophy speak for themselves (do they?) while poetry must be qualified? Has *poetry* never been a neutral word? Is it because the writer does not want us to get the wrong idea, that Paul might be a weak, sentimental loafer—perhaps a tad *feminine*?—who spends all day in a café, loafing? And they have a very good point there, because that's as much a clichéd portrait of a poetry-lover as anything in this ad. But most of all, what *is* fine poetry? Okay, in his apartment or, more likely, house, Paul has Shakespeare and Kierkegaard, Dickens and Marcus Aurelius— that's for sure. But what does his poetry collection look like? I've thought about this for a disproportionate amount of time. I think it means *The Divine Comedy*, Eliot, and Rilke. I think fine poetry in this context means *vintage* poetry, as in fine wine, poetry of long-established recognition. And there is nothing wrong with that. Nothing at all. I would wager the cost of a Coach bag there is not a mature poet writing today in English, including the most extreme antiestablishmentarian you can think of, who does not have all of those authors on the bookshelf. So why am I so upset by this little phrase *fine poetry*? And why do I want so badly to insert the words *madness, rack, and honey* in its place? I think it is because I do not know if Paul Einstein reads fine poetry for the madness, rack, and honey of it, or if he reads it because it is an accessory to a lifestyle of literature and philosophy—the bag that goes with the clothes. I think that the latter is what the written ad is trying to convey, but when I look at Paul's eyes, I think I see the madness, rack, and honey of it.

The phrase *madness, rack, and honey* came to me in a dream. And I want to tell you what the words mean to me, I want to publicly interpret my own dream, which consisted solely of these three words. Let us work backward, beginning with the word *honey*. Here is a famous Persian poem I love, originally written centuries ago in Farsi, told to me by an Iranian woman who could not remember the poet's name, except to say it was *not* Rumi, and that almost any Iranian, except herself, could identify the author. Still, after exhaustive searching, I can't find reference to this poem anywhere, so in my heart, I give it to the great Hafiz.

> I shall not finish my poem.
> What I have written is so sweet
> The flies are beginning to torment me.

It is so simple and clear: the "figurative" sweetness of the author's verse has become honey, causing "literal" flies to swarm on the page or in or around the author's head. This is truly the Word made flesh, the fictive made real, water into wine. That is the honey of poetry: the miracle of its transformation, which is that of creation: once there was a blank page—scary!—now there is something in its place that is attracting flies. Anyone who has not experienced the joy, pleasure, transport, and sweetness of writing poems has not written poems. If it has never once been fun for you, you probably haven't experienced what we talk about when we talk about poetry.

But let us return to the poem. There is a transformation in the poem from the figurative to the literal, without, of course, the poem ever leaving the figurative world of itself. Time has presumably passed in the poem, has just passed or is just beginning to pass—if you believe that the flies have gotten wind of the sweet verses and started to pursue them—and yet, being wholly a lyric poem of the moment, in which nothing happens on the scale of birth, love affairs, or death, how is it that we measure time in these three lines? I am talking about time as *event*, time as measurable in terms of what happened, our usual, quotidian way of measuring (some might say creating) time. And I am at once struck by what a perfect example the poem is regarding *metaphor as event*. Metaphor as time, the time it takes for an exchange of energy to occur. Metaphor is not, and never has been, a mere literary term. It is an event. *A poem must rival a physical experience* and metaphor is, simply, an exchange of energy between two things. If you believe that metaphor is an event, and not just a literary term denoting comparison, then you must conclude that a certain philosophy arises: the philosophy that everything in the world is connected. I'll go slowly here: if metaphor is not idle comparison, but an exchange of energy, an event, then it unites the world by its very premise—that things connect and exchange energy.

And if you extrapolate this philosophy further, you eventually cease to believe in separate realities. Why then do poets persist in insisting upon their separate realities (I know I insist on mine)? Because—goes the answer—it is also the nature of poetry to assert individual identity.

No, that's not true; I'm sorry but I chose the wrong words there. I should have said a very different thing; I should have said, "It is also the nature of poetry *to determine or affirm* one's relation to the incomprehensible condition of existence." I say "existence" because it is different than identity. I say "determine *or* affirm" because there is an option here: the great sculptor Giacometti once said, "I do not know whether I work in order to make something or in order to know why I cannot make what I would like to make." Perhaps when one makes something one affirms, and when one tries to make and knows they cannot (another kind of making) one determines. One determines that they cannot, one determines this by endlessly attempting.

"By the end of the nineteenth century, the German philologist Heymann Steinthal"—philology is the study of human speech as the vehicle of literature and as such sheds light on cultural history—"had concluded that language was not meant solely for communication. 'Language is self-awareness,' he said. 'That is, understanding oneself . . . as one is understood by another. One understands oneself: that is the beginning of language.'" (Russ Rymer, *The New Yorker*, April 13, 1992)

But self-awareness means many things, and one of the things it can mean, can come to mean, is that the self is aware that it is not distinct or separate. It is and it isn't; it is capable of both affirming and determining that it cannot affirm. I apologize for sounding obtuse. But I have been thinking—probably too hard—about this little poem that moves me so, and it caused me to remember a time in my life as a poet when I suffered a great crisis of metaphor. I will spare you the details of my agony, but I felt, for a while, that I was wasting my life making idle comparisons between things that could not and need not be compared. Recently I came across something so simply put it took my breath away. It's a remark originating with the Sung master Qingdeng, though there are many different versions of it, including this one, used by the Vietnamese monk Thich Nhat Hanh: "Before I began to practice, mountains were mountains and rivers were rivers. After I began to practice, mountains were no longer mountains and rivers were no longer rivers. Now, I have practiced for some time, and mountains are again mountains and rivers are again rivers." Metaphor doesn't actually exist, insofar as it does not reside in nature, but it exists insofar as it spontaneously arises in the human mind as a perceptual event. To conceive of things that don't exist is a *natural* act for a human being. My crisis passed but what stayed with me was the knowledge—implied, I think in the Buddhist saying—that these cycles will endlessly repeat themselves as long as we are alive. The *event* of metaphor, of figurative language and thought, will arise and subside, like any event. And our world is richer for it. Perhaps a little more complicated than it needs to be, but the presence of human beings on this planet has always complicated things—no one will deny that, not even terra firma herself.

> I shall not finish my poem.
> What I have written is so sweet
> The flies are beginning to torment me.

This poem *is* a physical experience. The poem, once begun, is so physical that it cannot realize itself: like an actual physical event (not like a poem at all) it must die, finish, or end *without completion*. Physical events, remember, only appear to reach completion—such as when we eat food or burn wood—all that energy is actually exchanged and transformed ad infinitum.

Enter the flies who feast. For the poem clearly reminds us that honey has complications—those flies are beginning to *torment* the poet. Torment, pain, torture, is what I mean by *rack*. A rack was a device engineered to induce pain, "an instrument of torture consisting of a frame having a roller at each end. The victim was fastened to these rollers by the wrists and ankles and had the joints of his limbs stretched by their rotation"—sometimes beyond endurance. The OED devotes three pages to the word *rack*, half of them practical, the other half painful:

want of proper economy or management; waste and de-
struction [as in rack and ruin]

that which causes acute suffering, mental or physical, also
the result produced by this; intense pain

to strain to the utmost

to examine searchingly, as by the application of torture

to pull or tear apart, to separate by force

to undergo strain or dislocation

to strain the meaning of, as in forced interpretation

to stretch or raise beyond the normal extent, amount or de-
gree

It is what poetry does to the world, what poets do with words, and what words will do to a poet. And that's the rack of it. And if you have never experienced the rack while working on a poem then you have never worked on a poem. Have you never put language in an extenuating circumstance with dangerous limits until an acute physical sensation results? Stanley Kunitz has said it gets harder and harder to write, not easier, because your standards and expectations—the limits of your endur-ance—become higher. He was thinking of the rack of it. And Elizabeth Bishop, in a letter, says the same thing. But Galway Kinnell has said, "the secret title of every good poem might be 'Tenderness'"; surely he was thinking of the honey of it. Frankenstein's monstrous and tender creature, in a remarkable passage, says, "Sometimes I wished to express my sensations in my own mode, but the uncouth and inarticulate sounds which broke from me frightened me into silence again." I am physically struck every time I ponder his words. It is a passage of torture, retreat, and nullification; but the "sometimes"— implying the stamina of more than once—and the "again" ("frightened me into silence *again*")—implying the multiplication of defeat *but also effort*—transform the passage into one with a clear echo of persistent, if faint, hope.

"You are a walking paradigm of the human condition—you think you know more about the universe than you actually do." "You are congenitally unable to do anything profitable." These astute remarks were made to me by someone who knows me well. And I am thankful for them, for they encourage me in ways he could not imagine and did not intend. John Ashbery, in an interview in the *Poetry Miscellany*, talks about wasting time: "I waste a lot of time. That's part of [the creative process]. . . . The problem is you can't really *use* this wasted time. You have to have it wasted. Poetry disequips you for the requirements of life. You *can't* use your time." In other words, wasted time cannot be filled, or changed into another habit; it is a necessary void of fomentation. And I am wasting your time, and aware that I am wasting it; how could it be otherwise? Many, many others have spoken about this. Tess Gallagher: "I sit in the motel room, a place of much passage and no record, and feel I have made an important assault on the Great Nothing." Gertrude

Stein: "It takes a lot of time to be a genius, you have to sit around so much doing nothing, really doing nothing." Mary Oppen: "When Heidegger speaks of boredom he allies it very closely with that moment of awe in which one's mind begins to reach beyond. And that is a poetic moment, a moment in which a poem might well have been written." The only purpose of this lecture, this *letter*, my only intent, goal, object, desire, is to waste time. For there is so little time to waste during a life, what little there is being so precious, that we must waste it, in whatever way we come to waste it, with all our heart. Charles Lamb: "A man can never have too much Time to himself, nor too little to do. Had I a little son, I would christen him NOTHING-TO-DO; he should do nothing. Man, I verily believe, is out of his element as long as he is operative."

Recently I found myself filling out a grant application by writing: "I seek an extended period of time, free from all distractions, so that I might be free to be distracted." Distraction is distracting us from distraction. Perhaps we wish to be distracted by the slightest nuances of being, thinking, feeling, or seeing. (We are drifting into the *madness* of it now.) Sometimes I think a poem is the "essence of distraction," which is certainly an oxymoron, since an essence is that which is most concentrated and distraction so wide; in a poem life distracts us from our lives, and only with the utmost of our concentration are we able to follow the exchange as it takes place. So the kind of distraction I am speaking of is one that leads to concentration, the concentrated form that is a poem. Students have complained that my lectures are always *written*; were I to spontaneously deliver a lecture on any subject whatsoever I can assure you it would be rehearsed and thus a sham. I write because I am a writer, and writing, in the course of my life, *has come to be more natural to me than speaking.* We are drifting into the *madness* of it now. Writing is my form of spontaneity and that is why I am writing you and not calling you on the phone. Recently a friend of mine designed a brochure describing an MFA program, a brochure intended to be mailed to prospective students. When my friend brought the proposed brochure to her institution's public relations artistic director—the designer ultimately responsible for the layout of the brochure—my friend was informed that because there were no images in it, the director herself would have to take charge and start over. Rule #1: No text is allowed on the cover—only images sell. "But," my friend said, "this brochure is intended for *writers* and they read texts; texts are important to them." "It doesn't matter," said the designer, "image *is* text. Image is the most powerful text at our disposal, and we intend to sell these brochures based on that premise." "But," my friend reminded her, "these brochures are *free.*" "No," said the director, "the brochures are paid for by the university and the university expects to be paid in kind by the students it admits. Nothing is free, and images have a higher face value than texts, that is the current free market value." This was followed by a long pause, after which she said, "I'm not

making this up. People have *written* about it, you know."
We have come to the madness of it now. We have come to the
madness, so let us descend. Here is a true story: In the mid-
dle of the holocaust that was Hiroshima, a Japanese soldier,
wounded, dazed, and wandering encountered the deformed
and dying without any overt emotion on his part, as he was
most likely, like thousands of others, in shock. He encountered
a group of young women, who at the sight of his wounds be-
gan to exclaim in horror and cry out. He later described this
moment: "It was my first contact with feminine emotion since
joining up, and it reminded me of a poem by the Chinese poet
Li Po that I had learned thirty years earlier at middle school.
For the first time, I realized that it was not just a piece of skill-
ful description, but a work of intense emotion." That in the
middle of nuclear carnage a man should remember a poem
from thirty years ago and have an insight into its nature—sim-
ply astounds me. Is it cruelly far-fetched—is it madness?—to
say that at this moment he was *wasting his time*? When the
world stops, when the power fails and the car won't start and
there's no water and your children are dead, what is there left
to do but to waste time? Madness is madness because it is in-
explicable. There's the madness of honey—a poem by Li Po!
after thirty years!—and there's the madness of the rack that was
Hiroshima. That they are capable of exchanging energy is
what I mean by madness. This is a true story: Shimazaki Tōson
(1872–1943), a Japanese writer, was determined to finish his

139

first novel, *The Broken Commandment*. An extreme and foolish belief in the supremacy of art was popular in Tōson's day, and he embraced it; he was determined to finish his book no matter what, so he drastically reduced his living expenses. As a result, his family suffered from malnutrition and three of his children, one by one, starved to death. Who would read this book? Thousands. And what of its title, *The Broken Commandment*? I believe we should as writers have an extreme and foolish belief in art—but not in the supremacy of art.

The madness of poetry is that it creates sweetness, so that the flies might come and eat till it is *gone*. "To endlessly make an end of things," says Paul Celan in a poem, and that's it, inexplicably and exactly. Miłosz: "The purpose of poetry is to remind us / how difficult it is to remain just one person." The madness is nowhere expressed so succinctly as when Yves Bonnefoy, the French poet, says, "Poetry is . . . the repudiation of poems." The context of this remark is one in which Bonnefoy explains how poetry asserts the unity of being by means of that which shatters it—language. If the flies keep on feasting, the honey will be gone. Then the flies will go away. And there will be nothing sweet. The poet has to either begin again—poor Creature!—or write a poem that goes on forever, and what a torment that would be! Even the long poem ends.

Pascal: "Runaway thought, I wanted to write it; instead, I write that it has run away."

You ask your teachers, "When will it end? When will it begin?'" You mean perhaps your writing life, some phase of it? You are *in* it. It began when you picked up a very thick pencil and learned to write your name on the widely ruled newsprint. It is a dot both *of* and *in* empty wasted time, and it can be *compared* to all the time that extends backward before your birth and forward after your death. In other words, your poems speak out of your wasted time the way your life speaks out of the wasted time of your nonlife, the time that surrounds your life span. One day you think like microbiologist Carl Woese, who uses this metaphor when speaking of the difficulties in distinguishing between microbes: "Imagine going out into the countryside and not being able to tell a snake from a cow from a mouse from a blade of grass. That was the level of our ignorance." Another day you think like Blake or Whitman and say: "Imagine going out into the countryside and not being able to tell a snake from a cow from a mouse from a blade of grass. That was the level of our wisdom."

As practitioners of poetry you are practitioners of madness, rack, and honey. You are mercy-givers who execute. You are executioners who show mercy. On May 13, 1619, in The Hague, there took place the public execution by decapitation of Jan van Olden Barneveldt, great politician of the newly founded Republic. As Zbigniew Herbert puts it: "The executioner led the condemned man to a spot where sunlight was falling and said, 'Here, Your Honor, you will have sun on your face.'"

Here is a beautiful Jewish custom: when a child is first introduced to books, a drop of honey is put on the cover and the child invited to step forward and lick it off so that he might know a rare sweetness awaits him.

In France in 1897 Émile Durkheim, the founder of modern sociology, published *Suicide: A Study in Sociology*. In it he observed a correlation between literacy and suicide. But I would be misleading you if I did not add and stress that Durkheim did not believe it was thought alone—literacy and education—that resulted in the fact that seven times as many Protestants committed suicide as Catholics (predominately Catholic countries had a higher rate of illiteracy) and fourteen times as many Jews —for behind literacy was the *breakdown of law* as expressed (formerly) by the Church. As an example of the necessity of a *combination* of factors, in Orthodox communities the suicide rate among literate Jews was practically nonexistent.

But still, a drop of honey is a powerful thing. It will draw flies. It is 1860. Mail is being transported by train throughout England, which has risen, through the grace and terror of coal and steel, as the most powerful country on earth. And the middle class is wasting its time on envelopes and stamps.

Charles Darwin picks up a pen and writes to Asa Gray: "But the more I think the more bewildered I become; as indeed I probably have shown by this letter."

MY EMILY DICKINSON

From first to last, there is no evidence that she laid any plans for the course of her life. She seems, above all, to have wished to avoid "doing something about" her life, and when, from time to time, the obligation was put to her, to make some sort of career for herself, and so prepare for her future, she tried to meet these demands, and failed.

MURIEL SPARK

A stone, a penny, a small bronze alien.

Emily's life is so well known as to need little introduction. She was born in 1818, the daughter of an Anglican parson in Haworth, Yorkshire. Painfully shy but with an extraordinary passion for the moors around her, she spent most of her life in Haworth. Brief spells at boarding school with her sister Charlotte, as a teacher in Halifax, and as a student in Brussels all ended in homesickness and a desperate longing for the freedom of the

143

moors. She spent the rest of her short life keeping house for her father, dying of tuberculosis in 1848.

She is often called the Sphinx of Literature, and when she was twelve years old, Emily Dickinson was born in America.

Two plastic champagne glasses, pink and purple larkspur, an ear.

As soon as I decided I wanted to write a lecture called "My Emily Dickinson" I discovered that the poet Susan Howe has a book called *My Emily Dickinson*. I thought about it for three hours, and decided to put the "My" in italics. *My* Emily Dickinson. I thought for another hour and decided that under no circumstances would I read Susan Howe's book. There were reasons. Knowing myself to whatever limited extent I do, I feared that if I read *My Emily Dickinson*, I would feel stupid, frustrated, inadequate, and completely incapable of "doing something about" it. Besides, I, who had learned to read at the age of five, and had never, ever, not for a single week, ceased to read some book or another from that time right on up to the very nearly present, had not read a single book in three years, being completely incapable of doing so, and felt not the slightest desire to do so now.

The next afternoon I happened upon a sidewalk sale of books, and there, gleaming up at me, gleaming and reaching, reaching and gleaming, speaking to me, speaking to me in a voice I barely recognized at first, because it was not a voice I knew, because it was a voice I had loved well but long ago, because it was my own voice all entwined with another's, was a voice telling me to pick up the book and begin reading. And it was like learning to read all over again. And it was poetry. And it was Emily Brontë.

COLD IN THE EARTH

Cold in the earth and the deep snow piled above thee!
Far, far removed, cold in the dreary grave!
Have I forgot, my Only Love, to love thee,
Severed at last by Time's all-wearing wave?

Now, when alone, do my thoughts no longer hover
Over the mountains on Angora's shore;
Resting their wings where heath and fern-leaves cover
That noble heart for ever, ever more?

Cold in the earth, and fifteen wild Decembers
From those brown hills have melted into spring—
Faithful indeed is the spirit that remembers
After such years of change and suffering!

145

Sweet Love of youth, forgive if I forget thee
While the World's tide is bearing me along:
Sterner desires and darker hopes beset me,
Hopes which obscure but cannot do thee wrong.

No other Sun has lightened up my heaven;
No other Star has ever shone for me:
All my life's bliss from thy dear life was given—
All my life's bliss is in the grave with thee.

But when the days of golden dreams had perished
And even Despair was powerless to destroy,
Then did I learn how existence could be cherished,
Strengthened and fed without the aid of joy.

Then did I check the tears of useless passion,
Weaned my young soul from yearning after thine;
Sternly denied its burning wish to hasten
Down to that tomb already more than mine!

And even yet, I dare not let it languish,
Dare not indulge in Memory's rapturous pain:
Once drinking deep of that divinest anguish,
How could I seek the empty world again?

All the while she was getting dressed she felt [the] poems
standing upright all over the room. She even kept an eye on

them in her dressingtable mirror, lest they escape into their natural vertical ascent.

J. D. SALINGER, "The Inverted Forest"

A lemon, a dime, a diamond ring, a parachute.

LIVING CONDITIONS

Emily Dickinson never lived alone for a single day of her life. She lived in a house with her father and mother and sister; after her parents died, she lived with her sister, Vinnie, until her own death, after which Vinnie lived alone. When we call her a recluse, we mean that after a certain point in her life, she ceased to leave the house, though it is documented by herself that she would many times go out at night, when there was no one else around.

"Though it is many nights, my mind never comes home."

Emily Brontë never lived alone for a single day of her life. She lived in a house in a remote and desolate setting that was of profound beauty to her. She lived in this house with her father, her aunt, her brother, and her two sisters, Charlotte and Anne. But like Emily, she was "a law unto herself"; she was "shy, often to the point of rudeness, with strangers." "If Emily wanted a book she might have left in the sitting-room she would dart in again without looking at any one, especially if any guest were present." There was a period in her life, after her aunt had died, when all three of her siblings were out in the world, attempting to make a life for themselves there, and she stayed at home, keeping house for her father. An old man in the village remembered seeing her coming down the lane on her way back from the moors, with a look "of holy rapture" on her face. After her beloved brother's death in the fall of 1848 she did not leave the house again until her own death in December, when her body was carried outside, to the graveyard that was "right there," just as Emily's was, in Amherst, though Emily's had to cross a dirt road on the side of the house, and be carried down through a meadow.

Anne Frank was a gregarious and popular girl who was housebound the last two years of her life because her family—herself, her mother, her father, and her sister Margot—went into hiding, in Amsterdam, with another family and a dentist, to escape the attention of the Nazis. After they were found out, she lived the last ten months of her life in three different prison camps, remaining, at the end, only with Margot.

Emily and Emily both lived in houses with views of a grave-
yard. Anne, at the end of her life, lived *in* a graveyard.

A white rose, a fortune-telling passion fish, ice cream for astro-
nauts.

EDUCATION

An educated person is one who can be reasonably called upon
to draw a conclusion. Alas, the only conclusion Emily and
Emily drew from being in school was that they would rather be
home, and so they left, and went home, and drew pictures of
dogs, and collected wildflowers.

Brontë wrote beneath one of her own poems: "I am more ter-
rifically and idiotically STUPID—than ever I was in the whole
course of my incarnate existence. The above precious lines are
the fruits of one hour's most agonizing labour between ½ past
6 and ½ past 7 in the evening of July—1836."

Her headmaster made this famous, infamous remark: "She
should have been a man—a great navigator. Her powerful rea-
son would have deduced new spheres of discovery from the
knowledge of the old; and her strong, imperious will would
never have been daunted by opposition or difficulty."

Anne Frank, on the other hand, was a terrific and popular student, whose education was cut short due to a strong, imperious will other than her own. In her school, it worked like this: every day you went to school and one of your classmates was missing; no one said anything, but the class continually thinned out until, at the end of the term, only one student arrived to take the final exams, took them alone, passed them, and was dismissed.

J. D. Salinger once remarked, "A writer, when he's asked to discuss his craft, ought to get up and call out in a loud voice just the names of the writers he loves," and then he listed the names of the authors he would call out, and on the list of sixteen names there is only one woman, and her name is Emily.

A sheaf of flowers from the florist with a thank-you note attached, a plastic fly, a nickel, an egg.

WINDOWS

Emily Dickinson oft looked out of her bedroom window, and many of her poems, if not her worldview, seem framed by this fact; so much has been made of this there is little I can add; to argue whether a window is the emblem of complete objectivity (removal and distance) or complete subjectivity (framing and viewpoint) is an argument without end, for every window has two sides, and they are subsumed in the window, the way yearning, a subsidiary of the window, is subsumed in both the object yearned for, and the subject of its own activity.

When Anne Frank was in hiding, one of her favorite activities was to look out the windows at night, which was the only time it was safe to do so. Her diaries record these yearning and rapturous moments, and even if the street was empty it was for her full of remembered life. Every time you so much as glance at the moon, you are looking at *the same moon* that Anne lingered on with so much heightened emotion.

In Emily's novel, Catherine's spiritghostself, that eidolon, haunts Heathcliff through the window (perhaps you remember the Kate Bush song from the 1980s with the desperate refrain, "Heathcliff! It's me, Cathy!") but Emily herself was not housebound and spent her days on the open moor—you could say she was moored by the moor—and I am reminded of a saying attributed to an old Benedictine: *Heather is going to spread its wings over the entire universe.* I'd like to propose the idea that Emily's ultimate window was the sky itself, immense expanse, the one that fueled her and that she seemed to see through and beyond. And indeed in her novel, Heathcliff spends his last days out in the open, cavorting among the heather with some unseen, but very real, presence. Unseen, but very real: not a bad definition of Anne Frank in hiding, or her diary, or Dickinson, that living diary.

A stick of gum wrapped in silver foil. A shard of glass.

NATURE

Is it because I haven't been outdoors for so long that I've become so smitten with nature? I remember a time when a magnificent blue sky, chirping birds, moonlight and budding blossoms wouldn't have captivated me. Things have changed since I came here. One night during the Pentecost holiday, for instance, when it was so hot, I struggled to keep my eyes open until eleven-thirty so I could get a good look at the moon, all on my own for once. Alas, my sacrifice was in vain, since there was too much glare and I couldn't risk opening a window. Another time, several months ago, I happened to be upstairs one night when the window was open. I didn't go back down until it had to be closed again. The dark, rainy evening, the wind, the racing clouds, had me spellbound; it was the first time in a year and a half that I'd seen the night face-to-face. After that evening my longing to see it again was even greater than my fear of burglars, a dark rat-infested house or police raids. I went downstairs all by myself and looked out the windows in the kitchen and private office. Many people think nature is beautiful, many people sleep from time to time under the starry sky, and many people in hospitals and prisons long for the day when they'll be free to enjoy what nature has to offer.

1400

What mystery pervades a well!
The water lives so far—
A neighbor from another world
Residing in a jar

Whose limit none have ever seen,
But just his lid of glass—
Like looking every time you please
In an abyss's face!

The grass does not appear afraid,
I often wonder he
Can stand so close and look so bold
At what is awe to me.

Related somehow they may be,
The sedge stands next the sea—

Where he is floorless
And does no timidity betray

But nature is a stranger yet;
The ones that cite her most
Have never passed her haunted house,
Nor simplified her ghost.

To pity those that know her not
Is helped by the regret
That those who know her, know her less
The nearer her they get.

SHALL EARTH NO MORE INSPIRE THEE

Shall Earth no more inspire thee,
Thou lonely dreamer now?
Since passion may not fire thee
Shall Nature cease to bow?

Thy mind is ever moving
In regions dark to thee;
Recall its useless roving—
Come back and dwell with me.

I know my mountain-breezes
Enchant and soothe thee still—

I know my sunshine pleases
Despite thy wayward will.

When day with evening blending
Sinks from the summer sky,
I've seen thy spirit bending
In fond idolatry.

I've watched thee every hour—
I know my mighty sway—
I know my magic power
To drive thy griefs away.

Few hearts to mortals given
On earth so wildly pine
Yet none would ask a Heaven
More like the Earth than thine.

Then let my winds caress thee—
Thy comrade let me be—
Since nought beside can bless thee
Return and dwell with me.

A plastic watch, a feather, some Kleenex.

SISTERS

Lavinia, Margot, Charlotte, and Anne: they are the *real* mysteries, with the exception of Charlotte, who was more famous than her sister Emily, so that everything we know about Emily comes to us through Charlotte and Charlotte's biographer.

But these are the real keepers of the keys.

In front of Dickinson's grave the earth is so trodden as to be bare dirt, while six inches to the left, in front of Lavinia's grave, the grass grows thick.

Lavinia lived with Emily her whole life long; there must have been trials.

Emily and Anne Brontë were especially close; they died within months of each other.

Margot and Anne? It is assumed that Margot died forty-eight hours before her sister, but who would know?
  "Abyss has no Biographer—
  Had it, it would not be Abyss—"

Nothing.

EMILY AND THE DRESSMAKER

Emily wore white dresses, made by a dressmaker. The one still retained in her bedroom, on a seamstress's dummy—actually the dress is an exact replica, since the original is being preserved in careful storage—is to the floor, tucked slightly at the waist but with no waist, made with vertical panels of a delicate but rather plain lace alternating with panels of unadorned cotton, long sleeves edged in this lace, a collar that can be curiously described as neither round nor square but somewhere in between, edged in this lace, and twelve white buttons down the front running about two-thirds the length of the dress, where there is a horizontal panel of fabric, edged in lace, from which fall flat square pleats all around to the floor. It is not an uncomfortable-looking dress—it looks rather like a nightgown—and it is patterned after a popular style of the day, nothing unusual or amiss.

With one exception. With what can only be at Emily's request, an outside pocket, completely outside, a workman's pocket, was added to the right-hand side of the dress, level with the sleeve of the right hand. And no curator, no costume historian, can come up with a reason for that pocket to be there, if not to hold something the wearer used with regularity and wanted to be always near—could it have been something to write with, and a piece of paper?

157

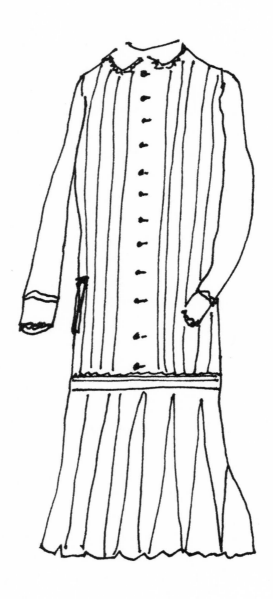

Emily in England, author of her own "death-impassioned, earth-enamoured" poems, the theorist whose work reveals a pantheistic, fatalistic philosophy complete unto itself—her sister said of Emily's ideas that "[they] strike my sense as much more daring and original than practical"—and the scholarly complaint to this day has been the same—none of her ideas function in the context of a traditional society—she who wrote, along with her siblings, from the earliest age, she who failed at being in the world as none other of her family did—unhappy as a student and a failure as a teacher, who once told her students she would rather be with her dog than with them—was a woman who, if you follow the life from first to last, as we do not have the time to do here, seems to hold one and only one image of herself—that of a creative writer. She simply never made any other plans. Every other thing she ever did was an act of familial coercion.

Having read Anne Frank's *Diary* I am convinced—not in an idle thoughtful way, but with the utter conviction of truth—that Anne, had she lived, would have become an author. It is the one thing that is clearly and persistently evident throughout the diary—she speaks of it herself, of her hopes and dreams of becoming a writer. Here is a child who writes an ode on the death of her fountain pen, which, as told in one of the journal's many unintended moments of wrenching irony, was accidentally cremated in the stove, "just as I would like to be someday!" she writes.

It is also evident that this young lady would have been earnestly involved with the fate of women everywhere, their individual and collective struggles for empowerment.

She would have been thirty-six in 1965.

Lilacs, a spool of thread, a book of matches, a mood ring.

THE BILLY COLLINS POEM

TAKING OFF EMILY DICKINSON'S CLOTHES

First, her tippet made of tulle,
easily lifted off her shoulders and laid
on the back of a wooden chair.

And her bonnet,
the bow undone with a light forward pull.

Then the long white dress, a more
complicated matter with mother-of-pearl
buttons down the back,
so tiny and numerous that it takes forever

before my hands can part the fabric,
like a swimmer's dividing water,
and slip inside.

You will want to know
that she was standing
by an open window in an upstairs bedroom,
motionless, a little wide-eyed,
looking out at the orchard below,
the white dress puddled at her feet
on the wide-board, hardwood floor.

The complexity of women's undergarments
in nineteenth-century America
is not to be waved off,
and I proceeded like a polar explorer
through clips, clasps, and moorings,
catches, straps, and whalebone stays,
sailing toward the iceberg of her nakedness.

Later, I wrote in a notebook
it was like riding a swan into the night,
but, of course, I cannot tell you everything—
the way she closed her eyes to the orchard,
how her hair tumbled free of its pins,
how there were sudden dashes
whenever we spoke.

What I can tell you is
it was terribly quiet in Amherst
that Sabbath afternoon,
nothing but a carriage passing the house,
a fly buzzing in a windowpane.

So I could plainly hear her inhale
when I undid the very top
hook-and-eye fastener of her corset

and I could hear her sigh when finally it was unloosed,
the way some readers sigh when they realize
that Hope has feathers,
that reason is a plank,
that life is a loaded gun
that looks right at you with a yellow eye.

Because poems are my life, a great many of them, both others'
and my own, piss me off. This is one of them.

So popular does this poem appear to be, that the title of Collins's newest book—the first collection of his work to be brought out in England—is titled *Taking Off Emily Dickinson's Clothes: Selected Poems*. Thank god for the other poems, many of which are wonderful.

What if this poem were called "Taking Off Toni Morrison's Clothes"?

Would I be less outraged, or more?

Well, we don't want to take off Toni Morrison's clothes, for starters, for the simple reason that we presume, since she has children, that somebody has already done that.

This poem is based entirely on the supposition that Dickinson is an icon of virginity and that it would be *fun* to do something with that idea, to be the *first* to do something with that idea. Poetry is subversive for a good reason, but for me it should never be rapacious, living on prey. Rape: to take away by force. Though the actions described in the poem couldn't be gentler, it is the *idea* here that uses force. I am fully aware that sexual acts involving or requiring passivity can be positive, erotic, and honoring. But I persist with my feeling that the woman in this poem does not want any of this to be happening—these words across the page are making her nervous—and that the speaker seems to be a stranger, and the audience rapt on the benches of a locker room.

But there is hope: Collins can't undress Emily because he doesn't even know where the buttons are! Women who live without partners or personal maids do not own dresses with innumerable tiny buttons running down the back—there is no way to put them on or take them off without assistance; Emily's buttons were in the front, where she could reach them.

I want to dress her for you, in the veils she loved and wrote about her whole life long, and I have chosen a dress by Versace; it is photographed in the desert, resting place of the Sphinx, and it has the wild wind of the moors all around it.

An envelope, addressed but otherwise empty, a piece of gum in silver paper, a packet of nasturtium seeds, and a button.

ACTS OF PRIVACY

She was a born celibate; in an earlier age, several centuries prior to the age in which she lived, she would have thrived in a convent. To think of her, or any other passionate celibate, as a frustrated spinster is wrong; she was completely capable of union in her own world, on her own terms; "a psychic hermaphrodite" Arthur Symons called her, one whose "passion without sensuousness" was intensely capable. It is a fact that despite writing what many merely remember as a great love story (it is that, and much more), she had in her own life not a single romantic attachment to another human being. It is often remarked that her characters seem sexless, and indeed they are;

Emily Dickinson in Versace

in her work the characters meet "on the grounds of passionate mutual identity"; sexual union would be beside the point—it is precluded, made impossible by the fact there is nothing to join: all has already been joined, or, to put it another way, all has been *samed* since the beginning of time.

298

Alone, I cannot be—
For Hosts—do visit me—
Recordless Company—
Who baffle Key—

They have no Robes, nor Names—
No Almanacs—nor Climes—
But general Homes—
Like Gnomes—

Their Coming, may be known
By Couriers within—
Their going—is not—
For they're never gone—

Dickinson had several passionate attachments in her lifetime, though none to fruition (whatever that is). And Anne spent much of her time in the annex making out with Peter, the son of the other family who hid with the Franks. And she spent much of the rest of her time writing about it in her diary, though these are precisely the passages that, in another act of privacy, were edited out by her father, and the diary found its original fame without them.

Emily was furious when her sister Charlotte discovered her personal poems. Emily was furious when Charlotte and their younger sister Anne made their famous trip to London to prove to their publishers that they were separate authors and Charlotte let slip the admission that actually there were *three*.

Dickinson was known as a poetess—to those who knew her—but still, imagine Lavinia's shock of having to discover and gather 1,775 little pieces of paper—some bound together—all stuffed in the drawers and empty spaces.

And how could it be, *how could it be*, that after the police stormed the apartment and arrested the Franks, and searched through everything, that one of them discovered the diary and, perhaps reading the ode to her fountain pen, threw it on the floor, moving on, leaving it there, scattered like trash, only to be picked up again later, by a friend, who saved it in the event—the hopeful unlikely event—one of them returned; and how could it be, *how could it be*, that out of eight people who lived and ate and hid together, only one would come back, in less than a year, only one, in less than a year.

Emily caught a cold at her brother's funeral. Her death is a legend, and nothing I can say will add or detract. Sullen, contemptuous, and inflexible? Or stoic, heroic, and noble? Dying of consumption in her thirty-first year, she refused all help, all attention, all concern, would take no medicine and see no doctor. She died not unlike . . . Heathcliff, who died not unlike . . . Catherine. According to the CliffsNotes:

> Heathcliff continues to seek solitude and only eats once a day. One night, a few days later, he leaves and is out all night. When he returns in the morning, Cathy [Catherine's daughter] remarks that he is actually quite pleasant. He rejects all food. When Nelly [the housekeeper] tries to encourage him to send for a minister, he scoffs at her and reminds her of his burial wishes. Later, Nelly sends for the doctor, but Heathcliff refuses to see him. The following night, Nelly finds Heathcliff's dead body.

Emily's father and sisters were barely allowed to mention her illness, despite the fact they could see she was dying; she could barely breathe, speak, or eat, but continued to do her daily round of household chores, going up and down the stairs. One day she lay down on the bench in the drawing room and told Charlotte she may send for a doctor if she'd like—and died that night.

Charlotte wrote to a friend:

> So I will not ask why Emily was torn from us in the fullness
> of our attachment, rooted up in the prime of her own days,
> in the promise of her powers; why her existence now lies
> like a field of green corn trodden down, like a tree in full
> bearing struck at the root.

It is a private question.

A thimble, an acorn, a quarter, and many, many daffodils.

LANGUAGE AND DEATH

Self-consciousness includes the consciousness of self-death.
Culturally, self-consciousness has evolved toward higher and
higher forms of literacy and with them more and more dwelling
on death. Literacy remarks not only on the death of an individ-
ual but on the death of societies and cultures, on environmen-
tal death and on the death of species who are not self-con-
scious, and it also remarks on the death of its own species as a
whole, the extinction of all self-consciousness (and all liter-
acy). At the same time, an individual who is highly literate, one
who reads and writes to an ever-advancing degree, dwells more

and more on his or her own death. Entrenched writers do this without question. From Virginia Woolf to Jacques Derrida, we have nothing but examples in every great work by every great writer in every great culture—and all cultures are great—and this *literacy of death* is self-consciousness in dialogue with its opposite, the absence of consciousness. But this dialogue (one in which the writer begins by *speaking* and more and more awakens to *listening*) takes time to develop and unfold; it takes time to come to terms with death.

Giorgio Agamben in *Language and Death* makes a point about this *literacy* of death. He says that to consent to language signifies acting in such a way that one voice is removed and another Voice is revealed, and along with it a new dimension of being and the mortal risk therein of nothingness. That's a rough and obtuse paraphrase, but here is the distinction he makes that I am interested in: "To consent to the taking place of language, to listen to the Voice, signifies, thus, to consent also to death, *to be capable of dying rather than simply deceasing*." (Italics mine.)

That Emily and Emily heard the Voice, and consented to it, and all the mortal risk therein, is clear to me: that they were capable of dying, rather than simply deceasing, is for me a truth. Emily in her second-story white bed in Amherst, *called back*, and Emily, on a wooden bench in the drawing room at Haworth, *called forth, died*; they died precisely because they had spent their lives—no matter how long, how short—in duration with this other Voice, which is a voice to which one *listens*.

> You do not need to leave your room. Remain sitting at your table and listen. Do not even listen, simply wait. Do not even wait, be quite still and solitary. The world will freely offer itself to you to be unmasked, it has no choice. It will roll in ecstasy at your feet.

KAFKA APHORISM

But what of Anne? Deceased. Anne did not die, though had she lived she would have been capable of it—of that I am certain. She expired, like an animal. She was denied her own capacity of dying because . . . because somebody else took it away from her, robbed her of it . . . by force. Not even a "body," not a somebody, but an enormous, a huge, an overwhelmingly large and pervasive Thought Machine Made Manifest on Earth.

Cause of death? The inner invasiveness of typhus, typhoid fever.
Cause of typhus? Unclean living conditions.
Cause of unclean living conditions? The outer invasiveness of an ideology lacking a circumference of love wide enough to shelter, among other things, a precocious, dark-eyed, fifteen-year-old girl in love with her fountain pen, and her hair.

"Genius is the ignition of affection—not intellect, as is sup-
posed—the exaltation of devotion, and in proportion to our ca-
pacity for that, is our experience of genius."

In another letter Emily wrote this: "Perhaps the whole United
States are laughing at me too! *I* can't stop for that. *My* business
is to love."

> I love you, with a love so great that it simply couldn't keep
> growing inside my heart, but had to leap out and reveal it-
> self in all its magnitude. *Yours,* ANNE FRANK

Anne Frank died of typhus at Bergen-Belsen in 1945. She met
up there with one of her best friends, her school chum Hannah
Pick-Goslar—"met up there"—I don't know how to call it;
what I mean is, at night, maybe three or four times, they met at
and talked through a wire wall stuffed with straw which divided
the camp. And Anne didn't cry out in the dark, "How can any-
one go on living after the barbarity of what has happened to
us here?" She didn't say that. She was a child, a writer, by vir-
tue of having written almost every day for two years, and a hu-
man being. She cried, saying, "I don't have any parents any-
more. . . . We don't have anything at all to eat here, almost noth-
ing, and we are cold; we don't have any clothes and I've gotten
very thin and they shaved my hair."

This morning I lay in the bathtub thinking how wonderful
it would be if I had a dog like Rin Tin Tin. *Yours,* ANNE
FRANK

> My solitaria
> Are the meditations of a central mind.
> I hear the motions of the spirit and the sound
> Of what is secret becomes, for me, a voice
> That is my own voice speaking in my ear.

> STEVENS, "Chocorua to Its Neighbor"

I hope I will be able to confide everything to you, as I have
never been able to confide in anyone, and I hope you will
be a great source of comfort and support. *Yours,* ANNE M.
FRANK

Loneliness ripens the eccentric, the daringly and estrang-
ingly beautiful, the poetic. But loneliness also ripens the
perverse, the disproportionate, the absurd, and the illicit.

> THOMAS MANN, *Death in Venice*

Perverse, disproportionate, absurd, and *illicit*—why, all those
words were used to describe *Wuthering Heights* when it first
came out—and even to this day, in regards to that masterpiece,
they are meaningful.

In nineteenth-century England, desks were fiercely private af-
fairs, almost like portable diaries—small and wooden, about
the size of a typewriter, with a slanted lid for writing, which
lifted up to reveal an empty space for storing papers; and they
locked, and you carried the key with you.

When Emily died and they unlocked her desk, it was found to
contain five reviews comparing her book unfavorably to Char-
lotte's best-selling *Jane Eyre*.

> The Frank girls were so emaciated. They looked terri-
> ble. . . . They had those hollowed-out faces, skin over bone.
> They were terribly cold. They had the least desirable places
> in the barracks, below, near the door, which was constantly
> opened and closed. You heard them constantly screaming,
> "Close the door, close the door," and the voices became
> weaker every day. . . .
>
> . . . I don't know which one was carried out earlier, Anne
> or Margot. Suddenly, I didn't see them anymore, so I had to
> assume that they had died. Look, I didn't pay any special at-
> tention to them because there were so many others who also
> died. When I didn't see them again, I assumed that they had
> died there, down there on that bunk. . . .
>
> The dead were always carried outside, laid down in front
> of the barracks, and when you were let out in the morning
> to go to the latrine, you had to walk past them. That was just

as dreadful as going to the latrine itself, because gradually everyone got typhus. In front of the barracks was a kind of wheelbarrow in which you could take care of your needs. Sometimes you also had to take those wheelbarrows to the latrine. Possibly it was on one of those trips to the latrine that I walked past the bodies of the Frank sisters, one or both—I don't know. . . . And then the heaps would be cleared away. A huge hole would be dug and they were thrown into it. That I'm sure of. That must have been their fate, because that's what happened with other people. I don't have a single reason for assuming it was any different for them than for the other women with us who died at the same time.

RACHEL VAN AMERONGEN-FRANKFOORDER

Beauty remains, even in misfortune. If you just look for it, you discover more and more happiness and regain your balance. A person who's happy will make others happy; a person who has courage and faith will never die in misery! *Yours,* ANNE M. FRANK

THE STARRY NIGHT SHALL TIDINGS BRING

> The starry night shall tidings bring:
> Go out upon the breezy moor,

Watch for a bird with sable wing,
And beak and talons dropping gore.

Look not around, look not beneath,
But mutely trace its airy way;
Mark where it lights upon the heath;
Then wanderer kneel thee down and pray.

What fortune may await thee there
I will not and I dare not tell;
But Heaven is moved by fervent prayer,
And God is mercy—fare thee well!

If I may, and I may, appropriate the words Vladimir Nabokov
used to explain the theme of his novel *Bend Sinister*, I will say
this: THE MAIN THEME OF THE COLLECTED POEMS OF
EMILY DICKINSON IS THE BEATING OF EMILY'S LOV-
ING HEART AND THE TORTURE AN IMMENSE TENDER-
NESS IS SUBJECT TO. Emily wrote in a letter, "All this and
more, though *is* there more? More than Love & Death? Then
tell me its name!"

Yellow snapdragons. A robin made of tin. A child's block with
the letter *E*. A pen. A pinecone. A tiny hat. An Australian coin.

CONNECTION

I don't know if there is a connection. If Anne the young writer had lived, I think she would have wondered the same thing—if there was a connection. Clearly Emily lived long enough to wonder if there was a connection. Sometimes we know there is a connection. Sometimes we wonder if there is a connection. And sometimes we know there is no connection, but we wonder then if one might be possible. It is all very confusing, to say the least.

> It is not recorded of any rose that it failed of its bee, though obtained in specific instances through scarlet experience. The career of flowers differs from ours only in inaudibleness. I feel more reverence as I grow for these mute creatures whose suspense or transport may surpass my own.

There were poets, and other authors, survivors, who, eventually, ceased writing after the Second World War. But I think it is very safe to say in general that writers did not cease writing after the war. Nor did the war end.

NO COWARD SOUL IS MINE

No coward soul is mine
No trembler in the world's storm-troubled sphere

I see Heaven's glories shine
And Faith shines equal arming me from Fear.

O God within my breast
Almighty ever-present Deity
Life, that in me hast rest
As I, Undying Life, have power in thee.

Vain are the thousand creeds
That move men's hearts, unutterably vain,
Worthless as withered weeds
Or idlest froth amid the boundless main

To waken doubt in one
Holding so fast by thy infinity
So surely anchored on
The steadfast rock of Immortality.

With wide-embracing love
Thy spirit animates eternal years
Pervades and broods above,
Changes, sustains, dissolves, creates and rears.

Though earth and moon were gone,
And suns and universes ceased to be
And thou wert left alone
Every Existence would exist in thee.

There is not room for Death
Nor atom that his might could render void
Since thou art Being and Breath
And what thou art may never be destroyed.

A paratrooper, a cork.

ABOUT HER WORDS

I have a friend named Kay Baker. She is sixty-five years old, a
retired teacher of literature who lives in Amherst and runs a
small, very small, antique store. As I have slowly gotten to know
her, I am amazed by her intelligence and fortitude, her kindness
and hardworking, responsible heart. She is very practical, and
down-to-earth—she is *sensible*. I am always somewhat smitten
by this particular manifestation of human nature, it being so far
removed from my own. The last conversation I had with her,
before Christmas, I told her I was working on this lecture, that
I was anxious, and, I feared, way in over my head, trying to talk
about Emily Dickinson, Emily Brontë, and Anne Frank in one
breath. And then I asked her what she thought they had in com-
mon. She was silent for a long while, and in that while I thought
of how much I *sensed* they had in common and how unable I
was to put my finger on it, to articulate it clearly or well; I could
show it, but not say it. And then she said it. She turned to me

with an easy smile on her face and said, "They have no experience of the world." They have no experience of the world. *They have no experience of the world.* She was right. And about her words I thought for the rest of the day. Deprivation is desire. Isolation is lust. To have no experience of the world—is passion for it. Not passion for *experience* of the world, but passion for the *world*. In fact, "to have no experience of the world" should be printed in all dictionaries everywhere as the definition of passion. They were magnificently prepared for nothing.

Once well-experienced in this world . . .

Had Anne lived to grow up . . .

Had Emily had buttons down the *back* of her dress . . .

Had Emily lived in a landscape with less wind, one that produced people instead of the yearning echoes of them, the hunting and haunted souls . . .

A voice within me is sobbing, "You see, that's what's become of you. You're surrounded by negative opinions, dismayed looks and mocking faces, people who dislike you, and all because you don't listen to the advice of your own better half." Believe me, I'd like to listen, but it doesn't work, because if I'm quiet and serious, everyone thinks I'm putting on a new act and I have to save myself with a joke, and then I'm not even talking about my own family, who assume I must be sick, stuff me with aspirins and sedatives, feel my neck and forehead to see if I have a temperature, ask about my bowel movements and berate me for being in a bad mood, until I just can't keep it up anymore, because when everybody starts hovering over me, I get cross, then sad, and finally end up turning my heart inside out, the bad part on the outside and the good part on the inside, and keep trying to find a way to become what I'd like to be and what I could be if ... if only there were no other people in the world. *Yours,* ANNE FRANK

A piece of coal, a candle stub, a chrysanthemum.

THE END

In the end, I have said very little about my Emily Dickinson. I would prefer not to, said Bartleby. My Emily Dickinson is nobody's business but my own. I will not share her with anyone. I would no more tell you about my relationship with her poems than I would tell you about a love affair. If she is yours, I hope you feel the same way. The little I can and will divulge is this: she possessed Language, and because of it—not *for* it, but *because* of it—she died, and did not simply decease. That is less common, and more rare, than one might think—to die. But she has a common grave, and I like to go there and leave things, and when I do, I see that many other people have done the same.

A small gargoyle, a rubber heart, an old key, a guitar pick, a sequin, a sprig of heather, and a piece of hair.

> "Now you can tell how great
> must be the love that burns in me
> when it escapes my mind that we are empty
> and I treat a shade as a solid thing."
>
> DANTE, *Purgatorio*

A doorknob.

SOMEONE READING A BOOK IS A
SIGN OF ORDER IN THE WORLD

When I was twenty-five I began to keep a monthly list of the books I read. Over time it became obvious that although some months I didn't read at all, and other months I read eight or nine books, on the average I read five books a month, or sixty books a year. Assuming this was more or less true from the time I was ten and began to read regularly—I know that in high school I was required to read a book a week and in college even more—I can calculate that I have probably read 2,400 books in my life, which may well be more than people read on average, but in light of all the books there actually are, or in light of even another fact—that in the year 2000, 200,000 books were published—it is a raindrop (though a very human one). Out of those 2,400 books I probably remember two hundred, or 8 percent. If asked to list them, I might not even get that far. What I want to know is: is all this proportional, or does it reach some point where it no longer is? In other words, if someone has read sixty books in his life, can he remember them all, or only five of them? And is there anyone out there who has read only six books and forgotten them all? Doesn't that seem unlikely? Am I a superfluous person because I have read more than I can possibly process, like an intake of food the body doesn't need, or am I a superfluous person because I have gone out and bought myself a new calculator?

When I was forty-five years old, I woke up on an ordinary day, neither sunny nor overcast, in the middle of the year, and I could no longer read. It was at the beginning of one of those marvelous sentences that only Nabokov can write: "Mark felt a sort of delicious pity for the frankfurters ..." In my vain attempts I made out *felt hat*, *prey*, *the city of Frankfort*. But the words that existed so I might read them sailed away, and I was stranded on a quay while everything I loved was leaving. And then it was I who was leaving: a terror seized me and took me so high up in its talons that I was looking helplessly down on a tiny, unrecognizable city, a city I had loved and lived in but would never see again. I needed reading glasses, but before I knew that, I was far far away.

The book I was reading I was rereading. Because some time before that terrible day I had reached a juncture in my reading life that is familiar to those who have been there: in the allotted time left to me on earth, should I read more and more new books, or should I cease with that vain consumption—vain because it is endless—and begin to reread those books that had given me the intensest pleasure in my past, books I had all but forgotten in their details, but loved in the shadows they cast over me, the moods created by the very thoughts of them. And there was curiosity, too, the curiosity of revisiting and remeeting. Some gigantic memory might strike me as being rather small in the flesh, or the altogether unremembered might strike me dead at a glance. It is not like returning to places; we don't find ourselves, in the fourth chapter of *Madame Bovary*, searching for the bakery that is no longer there. Our curiosity is always self-directed: Have *I* changed? Do I still love the Makioka sister who has diarrhea on the train in the last sentence? *Is* that the last sentence? Was I too young when I read Proust?

I read Proust when I was in my twenties. I rationed that novel by reading one volume a year. I had a friend whose father was a man of letters, and he had said that once you read Proust there was no reason to ever read again, you had reached the end of reading, and as I was young and respected him enormously, I was afraid to finish that book, my incessant and increasing love for it was all wrapped up in this grotesque fear that my inner life was coming to an end before it had even begun. Which was correct. That's the cookie, isn't it? As for the larger statement—once you read Proust there is no reason to read again—I found that, like most things, it was both true and untrue.

There is the old story of Somerset Maugham reading Proust while crossing the desert by camel, and to lighten his load he tore out each page after reading both sides and let it fall behind him—one wants to say the wind was involved, but on most days there was no wind. With or without wind, who had a more memorable reading experience, Somerset Maugham or the one who came after him, the one who found and read a page here, a page there, in some strange new order with stellar gaps? Is this not a truer experience of *In Search of Lost Time* than of *Remembrance of Things Past*?

Pollard: to cut back a tree to its trunk so as to induce a dense growth of foliage at its head. But it also means a hornless animal of a usually horned kind.

To reread a book is to make a pollard of it.

Is there a right time to read each book? A point of developing consciousness that corresponds with perfect ripeness to a particular poet or novel? And if that is the case, how many times in our lives did we make the match? I heard someone say, at a party, that D. H. Lawrence should be read when one is in their late teens and early twenties. As I was nearing thirty at the time, I made up my mind never to read him. And I never have. Connoisseurs of reading are very silly people. But like Thomas Merton said, one day you wake up and realize religion is ridiculous and that you will stick with it anyway. What love is ever any different?

There was one book I read not only at the right age but also on the right afternoon, in the right place, at the right angle. I read *The Waves* on an island, on a plotless day, when I was twenty-two years old, sitting on a terrace from which I could see in the distance the ocean, and the horizon where it met the sky and the changing light that played there as the sun climbed to its zenith and descended again while I thumbed the pages and my blood pressure washed up and down with the words. *The Waves* is not one of my favorite books. But my memory of reading it is. I was very silly when I was young. I have that to be thankful for.

I was very serious when I was in high school. I must have been, for my two memorable reading experiences from that time are very serious indeed. Both of them took place, of all places, in the classroom. Some English periods we were assigned to simply sit and read silently. We were reading *The Return of the Native* (or was it *The Mayor of Casterbridge*?), our silent minds on different pages. I was not in the classroom of course; I was in Wessex. And there came the inevitable Wessexian moment: a letter, *the* letter, *the one that would make everything okay*, being slipped under a closed door got wedged under the carpet on the other side, where no one would see it. This was awful. What happened then I could not foresee: my arm threw the book as hard as it could across the quiet room. Mrs. Pacquette asked me to explain myself. All I could do was stammer that it was *awful, awful, awful*. She supposed I meant the book. I did not. I meant the thing that was going to happen in the book, because no one was going to read the letter. Therefore I was not going to read the book. In retrospect I see that even then I was engaged in the mirrored erotics of this compulsive activity, reading. Hardy grew up to be one of my beloveds, as did Kafka, to whom it happened next. "The Burrow" was in one of our textbooks. As the class sat reading silently, the silence seemed different. I was infuriated by my inability to understand what was happening in the story. What was happening? Deep inside myself I could not believe that anyone else was actually reading. I was convinced that a mistake had been made, that the printing plates—for I pictured them as such—had gotten smashed and all mixed up. There was a mistake. Was I the only one who noticed? Hadn't the teachers bothered to read the story? Their secret was out! There was a very special kind of attention that only I was able to pay to the story—it was absurd. And then I had a moment of doubt. *Who wrote this?* Perhaps *he* was the mistake, and not the story. I sat in the silent classroom and I heard all kinds of things—I heard the nonticking clock tick, and the sweat beginning to form on my body, and the window glass was about to break into pieces. The pencil sharpener on the wall was salivating. I flipped to the back of the book where there were brief paragraphs about each of the authors, who they were, where they came from, when they wrote. Yes, I was certain now, the mistake was not in the story but in its author. There was a mistake in the man. There had to be a mistake in the man because I was told where and when he wrote but not *why*. And of all the stories in our book, this was the one that remained starved and unfed unless I learned *why* he wrote it at all. I decided to hate the author. I decided to hate the author because he made me feel as if all my life I had been waiting for something to happen, and it was happening and it was not going to happen. It was many years before I understood that this was the secret labyrinth of reading, and there was a secret tunnel connecting it to my life.

I find nothing in my life that I can't find more of in books. With the exception of walking on the beach, in the snowy woods, and swimming underwater. That is one of the saddest journal entries I ever made when I was young.

Reading is hazardous. Here is a true story that proves it: a Chinese student, having read *The Scarlet Letter*, saw an American in China wearing a high school letter jacket with the letter *A* on the front and said, *I know what that means.*

Hazardous even to the initiated: Recently I was reading the notebooks of the Greek poet George Seferis (1900–1971). I was also reading, for the first and last time in my life, my own private journals, which I began writing when I was sixteen and ceased to write when I was forty. As is my habit, I was copying selected passages from the Seferis into a notebook. Later that evening I began reading a journal I kept twenty years ago. In it, I was reading the notebooks of the poet George Seferis (1900–1971) and had copied into the journal by hand my favorite passage, which was identical with the passage I had copied earlier in the day, believing completely that I had never encountered it before: *But to say what you want to say, you must create another language and nourish it for years and years with what you have loved, with what you have lost, with what you will never find again.*

Altogether, I think we ought to read only books that bite and sting us. If the book we are reading doesn't shake us awake like a blow to the skull, why bother reading it in the first place? So that it can make us happy, as you put it? Good God, we'd be just as happy if we had no books at all; books that make us happy we could, in a pinch, also write ourselves. What we need are books that hit us like a most painful misfortune, like the death of someone we loved more than we love ourselves, that make us feel as though we had been banished to the woods, far from any human presence, like a suicide. A book must be the ax for the frozen sea within us. That is what I believe.

KAFKA IN A LETTER, 1904

What kind of book would that dazzling human animal Consuelo sit down to read after she had finished washing the blood off her hands and had hidden once more her machete in the piano?

STEVENS IN A LETTER, 1948

There was an anthology, a fat Bantam paperback with a glossy white cover (like *The White Album*) and something like an abstracted dove embossed on it, called *Modern European Poetry*, and it was mine, my joy and my solace when I was in high school; whatever problems I had with Hardy and Kafka in the classroom vanished in the solitude of my bedroom, which I shared with Rilke, Lorca, Montale, Éluard, Ritsos—everybody was in that book, I didn't have another book I loved half so much, I must have read it a hundred times, and then I grew up, and went out into the world, and promptly lost it.

Once this thought crossed my mind: every time an author dies, out of respect a word should also pass out of being. A word the author loved and used repeatedly in writing—that word should be his and die with him. Nabokov: *quiddity*. But who should decide? The one who passes or the one who is left bereft? And who is the real widow? It is language herself, and her decision is clear: she does not want one of her children to throw herself into the grave pit of an old man. *Quiddity*: the essence of a thing; also, a trifling point, a trivial, inessential thing.

I've often thought that in acting classes the students should perform scenes in which they are simply reading. And I've wondered what subtle—or remarkable—differences there might be among the outward appearances of reading different books. Early Tolstoy versus late Tolstoy might be an advanced assignment—that kind of thing. Or would they all appear the same? The outward idleness, almost slumbering, that does nothing to convey the inner activity, whether it be reverie, shock, hilarity, confusion, grief. We don't often watch people very closely when they read, though there are many famous paintings of women reading (none that I know of of men) in which a kind of quiet eroticism takes place, like that of nursing. Of course, it is we who are being nursed by the books, and then I think of the reader asleep, the open book on his or her chest.

I don't know what my face conveyed while I was reading *Seven Pillars of Wisdom* by T. E. Lawrence. It takes place in the desert and I read it in front of a woodstove during a four-day blizzard. I suppose it is very odd that I single this book out instead of, say, Lautreamont's *Les Chants de Maldoror*, an equally violent, anguished book, but I do. I've always defended *Pillars* as an unspeakable achievement in literature and disorder. In blood and displacement and an English lost in sand. Read only the first chapter and you will have read the human fate. I am exaggerating, of course. Like a book.

There is a world that poets cannot seem to enter. It is the world everybody else lives in. And the only thing poets seem to have in common is their yearning to enter this world.

For years I planned a theoretical course called Footnotes. In it, the students would read a footnoted edition of a definitive text—I thought it might as well be *The Notebooks of Malte Laurids Brigge*—and proceed diligently to read every book mentioned in the footnotes (or the books by those authors mentioned) and in turn all those mentioned in the footnotes of the footnoted books, and so on and so on, stopping only when one was led back, by a footnote, to *The Notebooks of Malte Laurids Brigge*.

The burrow has probably protected me in more ways than I thought or dared think while I was inside it. This fancy used to have such a hold over me that sometimes I have been seized by the childish desire never to return to the burrow again, but to settle down somewhere close to the entrance, to pass my life watching the entrance, and gloat perpetually upon the reflection—and in that find my happiness —how steadfast a protection my burrow would be if I were inside it.

KAFKA, "The Burrow"

I had recently one of the most astonishing experiences of my reading life. On page 248 in *The Rings of Saturn*, W. G. Sebald is recounting his interviews with one Thomas Abrams, an English farmer who has been working on a model of the temple of Jerusalem—you know, gluing little bits of wood together —for twenty years, including the painstaking research required for historical accuracy. There are ducks on the farm and at one point Abrams says to Sebald, "I have always kept ducks, even as a child, and the colours of their plumage, in particular the dark green and snow white, seemed to me the only possible answer to the questions that are on my mind." It is an odd thing to say, but Sebald's book is a long walk of oddities. I did not remember this passage in particular until later the same day when I was reading the dictionary, where I came upon the meaning of the word *speculum*: (1) an instrument inserted into a body passage for inspection; (2) an ancient mirror; (3) a medieval compendium of all knowledge; (4) a drawing showing the relative position of all the planets; and (5) a patch of color on the secondary wings of most ducks and some other birds. Did Sebald know that a compendium of all knowledge and a duck's plumage were one and the same? Did Abrams? Or was I the only one for whom the duck passage made perfect, original sense? I sat in my chair, shocked. I am not a scholar, but for the imaginative reader there can be discoveries, connections between books, that explode the day and one's heart and the long years that have led to the moment. I am a writer, and the next step is inevitable: I used what had been revealed to me in my own writing.

We are all one question, and the best answer seems to be love—a connection between things. This arcane bit of knowledge is respoken every day into the ears of readers of great books, and also appears to perpetually slip under a carpet, utterly forgotten. In one sense, reading is a great waste of time. In another sense, it is a great extension of time, a way for one person to live a thousand and one lives in a single life span, to watch the great impersonal universe at work again and again, to watch the great personal psyche spar with it, to suffer affliction and weakness and injury, to die and watch those you love die, until the very dizziness of it all becomes a source of compassion for ourselves, and for the language which we alone created, without which the letter that slipped under the door could never have been written, or, once in a thousand lives—is that too much to ask?—retrieved, and read. Did I mention supreme joy? That is why I read: I want everything to be okay. That's why I read when I was a lonely kid and that's why I read now that I'm a scared adult. It's a sincere desire, but a sincere desire always complicates things—the universe has a peculiar reaction to our sincere desires. Still, I believe the planet on the table, even when wounded and imperfect, fragmented and deprived, is

worthy of being called whole. Our minds and the universe—
what else is there? Margaret Mead described intellectuals as
those who are bored when they don't have the chance to talk
interestingly enough. Now a book will talk interestingly to you.
George Steiner describes the intellectual as one who can't read
without a pencil in her hand. One who wants to talk back to the
book, not take notes but make them: one who might write,
"The giraffe speaks!" in the margin. In our marginal existence,
what else is there but this voice within us, this great weirdness
we are always leaning forward to listen to?

In the 2001 Kentucky Derby, which I watched live on televi-
sion, Keats ran against Invisible Ink. There was no way I was
going to miss this race. But I waited in vain for one of the
sportscasters to mention that Keats was an English poet whose
only surviving descendants must live in Kentucky, where his
older brother had immigrated, remained healthy and had chil-
dren, and I waited in vain for someone to mention the poet's fa-
mous epitaph—*Here lies one whose name was writ in water*—
and its curious connection to Invisible Ink. In all the network,
that great kingdom of connection, what had been read or re-
membered? It was as sad as a horse's eye. Keats lost. Invisible
Ink placed second, but had he been third, he would have
showed.

The only bumper sticker worth having: OBLOMOV FOR PRES-IDENT.

Against the Grain. Nightwood. The Dead. Notes from Under-ground. Fathers and Sons. Eureka. The Living. The Marriage of Heaven and Hell. The Sun Also Rises. Luminous Debris. Childish Things. The Wings of the Dove. The Journal of an Understanding Heart. Wuthering Heights. One Hundred Years of Solitude. Tristes Tropiques. The Tale of Genji. Black Sun. Deep Ocean Organisms Which Live Without Light. The Speeches of a Dictator. The Fundamentals of Farming. The Physics of Lift. A History of Alchemy. Opera for Idiots. Let-ters from Elba. For Esmé—with Love and Squalor. The Walk. The Physiology of Drowning. Physicians' Desk Reference. Bleak House. The Gospel according to Thomas. A Biography of Someone You've Never Heard Of. Forest Management. Black Lamb and Grey Falcon. Travels in Arabia Deserta. The Collected Works of Paul Valéry. A Book Written in a Language You Do Not Understand. The Worst Journey in the World. The Greatest Story Ever Told. A Guide to Simple First Aid. The Art of Happiness.

REMARKS ON LETTERS

I think it extraordinary that letters are called *letters*, the name of that small denomination with which we build our words. A letter is a sound and a sound is a voice and a voice to which we attach meaning—or significance—is a life.

> A Letter always feels to me like immortality because it is the mind alone without corporeal friend.

EMILY DICKINSON

I do not know how many letters I have written or sent by mail in my life, but I know of only two that did not reach their destination. When I was twenty-two I sent two postcards to two friends in Mexico, which they never received. The postcards were photographs from the American Civil War—the dead bodies of soldiers strewn across a battlefield—and though I no longer remember what the messages were, I have always thought twice about the fact they ended up in the office of dead letters, that remote and obscure place of absolute silence, which for me is a more accurate description of hell than a writhing inferno of animated anguish.

A mass grave, a pile of abandoned bones, undiscovered, unknown, unopened, undelivered, ditched, sealed, forgotten.

Much like the earth itself. On the surface of which things happen, ceaseless occurrence gives way to ceaseless occurrence, and things do have their births, and their beginnings.

The novel, for instance. The rise of the English novel in the eighteenth century was the direct result of four forces that are related: the rise of science and the decline of fatalistic religious feeling, by which an ordinary life, one's personal fate, was suddenly imbued with a sense of open uncertainty; economic shifts resulting in the rise of a middle class, which is always a rise in literacy, a rise in leisure time (to read, to travel), and a rise in uncertainty—the lower class can rise into the arms of the middle class, the upper class can fall into its jaws; a mania for travel and the means for it, the desire to have "adventures," to know about other lands and other peoples, if not firsthand, then through the experiences of others; and improvements, vast, in the postal system, resulting in a mania for letters, a veritable letter-craze.

Hence one contender for the first modern British novel is Samuel Richardson's *Pamela*, written in 1740 in the form of letters, a book in which a member of the working class marries a member of the ruling class. In its essence then, the English novel as a form originates from a sense of uncertainty: what will happen to these characters?

Three hundred years later we ask: what will happen to the world? In what form will the novel survive, in what form will the poem survive, in what form will letters survive?

Whenever I deposit a letter in my mailbox, whenever I drop an envelope into the brass slot at the post office—and this is intensified tenfold if I resort to a public mailbox at a street corner, which I try in my fear to avoid but am often reduced to—I am overcome with uncertainty: I think it uncertain that this piece of paper will ever survive the circuitous route to its destination, will ever arrive; I always hold my breath and sometimes close my eyes.

How does the e-mail travel through cyberspace to its destination? How can I hold something in my hand and hear a voice halfway around the world?

The advent of the telephone caused a considerable drop in personal letters. It has been argued that the rise of e-mail is a

revival of literate communication. I am fascinated by the new
set of signs and symbols e-mailers employ to denote emotional
resonance in their clickings: I am told there is a symbol that lets
the reader know the communication is ironic.

The dumbing down of the public sphere is truly awe-inspir-
ing.

Insert here lecture on postage stamps, lecture on envelopes,
lecture on the folding of paper.

Letter 3. Summer 1861. Manuscript: A 828. Two sheets of
stationery, each comprising two leaves 202 × 127 mm. The
paper is laid, cream with a blue rule, and embossed with a
decorative frame (13 × 11 mm.) containing a queen's head
above the letter L. The manuscript has been folded hori-
zontally into thirds.

Written in ink, revised in ink and pencil, this letter was
begun as a final draft suitable for sending. . . . Although she
continued on, the draft became intermediate on the fourth
page. There, near the top, in ink, she cancelled the word
"our"; further down, knowing that this would now not be a
final copy, she wrote the alternative wording "remember
that" above the line, also in ink. All the other revisions were
in pencil, made after she had finished with pen. She went
back through the whole letter, making many changes, and

added two passages at the end, one marked for insertion in the midst of a change on the second page, the other unmarked.

R. W. FRANKLIN IN

The Master Letters of Emily Dickinson

Personally, I think the two added passages at the end, which go together, were the beginnings of a poem she had written herself into, in her letter-craze; in her letter-craze of course she had been a poet all along—how could she not be?—but it seems to me she did not apprehend this fact, in her letter-craze, until the end, when a recognizable poem begins, and the letter stops short, the draft dies at the exact moment the no-bird soars into the ether.

The bird's nest burns up.

Smoke signals are perhaps the most beautiful form of the letter ever to evolve. For what is a letter, but to speak one's thoughts at a distance? Which is why poems and prayers are letters. The origins of poems, prayers, and letters all have this in common: urgency. They each originate in the pressing need to make a message directed at something unnear, that the absence of the unnear be made to appear present—that the presence of absence be palpably felt—that consciousness create consciousness. There are a hundred ways to try and speak precisely about this act; suffice it to say that it is a very powerful act.

The earliest extant letters in Western culture are messages sent from emperors and kings to their generals on the battlefield, and what is remarkable about these acts is that they constitute a round of gossip at the point of death, or gossip surrounding the point of death, which will always include, one hopes, words of encouragement and the courage inside it.

Extrapolate this history to include urgent messages exchanged *between* rulers, trying to avoid the onset of slaughter. Extrapolate this history to include letters written by soldiers preparing to die in battle—letters composed with the express purpose of conveying one's last words to one's family. Such letters have always been found on the bodies of dead soldiers.

On September 11, 2001, when the two towers of the World Trade Center collapsed, many people were haunted by the last-minute cell phone calls made by those about to perish. Those recordings are not what haunt me. What haunts me is the image of smoke, rolling mountains of billowing combustion on top of which dance thousands of pieces of paper, suspended in the wind created by the fathomless incineration nothing escaped—except the paper, those thin, meaningless, and disposable sheets.

Once I witnessed a windstorm so severe two 100-year-old trees were uprooted on the spot. The next day, walking among the wreckage, I found the friable nests of birds, completely intact and unharmed on the ground. That the featherweight survive the massive, that this reversal of fortune takes place among us— that is what haunts me. I don't know what it means.

I took one of those nests and carefully pinned it to a wall in my study. Then I pinned a folded handwritten letter inside the nest. I did this years ago. I don't know why I did it. I just did it.

Nothing I understand haunts me. Only the things I do not understand have that power over me.

I get so very tired of having to talk about literature. I didn't begin writing because I wanted to sit in a room and talk about the construction of subjectivity in Wordsworth and Ashbery; I began writing because I had made friends with the dead: they had written to me, in their books, about life on earth and I wanted to write back and say *yes, house, bridge, river, hair, no, maybe, never, forever.*

The greatest lesson in writing I ever had was given to me in an art class. The drawing instructor took a sheet of paper and held up a pencil. She very lightly put the pencil on the piece of paper and applied a little pressure; by bringing her hand a little ways in one direction, she left a mark upon the paper. "That's all there is to it," she said, "but it's a miracle. Once there was nothing, and now there's a mark."

Sad to me is the demise of the telegram, because even if the message was utterly *mundane*, it always *seemed* urgent because of the standard format of printing the word STOP between sentences, which made you catch your breath as if your heart were stopping. In writing, frequent stops can convey a sense of urgency better, I think, than an unstopped stream of consciousness in which nothing but undifferentiated time passes. Unless, of course, one is actually—psychically—caught up in that horrific flow from which there is no escape, as a few great writers have actually been. Here is Kafka writing about the delivery of a message, in his story "The Great Wall of China":

> The Emperor, so it runs, has sent a message to you, the humble subject, the insignificant shadow cowering in the remotest distance before the imperial sun; the Emperor from his deathbed has sent a message to you alone. He has commanded the messenger to kneel down by the bed, and has whispered the message to him; so much store did he lay on it that he ordered the messenger to whisper it back into his ear again. Then by a nod of the head he has confirmed

that it is right. Yes, before the assembled spectators of his death—all the obstructing walls have been broken down, and on the spacious and loftily mounting open staircases stand in a ring the great princes of the Empire—before all these he has delivered his message. The messenger immediately sets out on his journey; a powerful, an indefatigable man; now pushing with his right arm, now with his left, he cleaves a way for himself through the throng; if he encounters resistance he points to his breast, where the symbol of the sun glitters; the way is made easier for him than it would be for any other man. But the multitudes are so vast; their numbers have no end. If he could reach the open fields how fast he would fly, and soon doubtless you would hear the welcome hammering of his fists on your door. But instead how vainly does he wear out his strength; still he is only making his way through the chambers of the innermost palace; never will he get to the end of them; and if he succeeded in that nothing would be gained; he must next fight his way down the stair; and if he succeeded in that nothing would be gained; the courts would still have to be crossed; and after the courts the second outer palace; and once more stairs and courts; and once more another palace; and so on for thousands of years; and if at last he should burst through the outermost gate—but never, never can that happen—the imperial capital would lie before him, the center of the world, crammed to bursting with its own sediment. Nobody could fight his way through here even with a message from a dead man. But you sit at your window when evening falls and dream it to yourself.

Once, as an adolescent, I stood in a grand, turn-of-the-century, high-ceilinged foyer, with an elaborate staircase behind me, a staircase with a black iron banister in the shape of vines, and the walls were a warm yellow-gold, and I inserted my key into a little brass mailbox and out fell a brown letter, and the sight of the hand (that beautiful term we use for handwriting) caused me to physically stagger, and then swoon, sway; just to receive it, unopened, unread, just to stand there and see it and hold it in my hands! Only now, thirty years later, do I understand what a miracle that moment was, that I was its destination and it had arrived. If I die tonight, that moment is blessed and without regret; very rarely in life are prayers thus answered. That this scene repeated itself several times in my life leaves me speechless.

And how pitiful I am, how wretched and deserving of your crudest sympathy, that I have experienced the countermovement of this moment, standing by the side of the road under a great elm, in a cloud of dust from a passing car, with a letter in my hands that caused me to collapse in pain and shock and acutest anguish. If I die tonight, these moments—for this scene, too, was repeated—will thankfully disappear from my consciousness. Very often in life our prayers are denied, re-pelled, ground to the ground, sent back to the ear unheard.

Once I saw a man beating his mailbox with his bare hands.

Northamptonshire County, General Lunatic Asylum, North-ampton, England:

March 8th 1860

Dear Sir

I am in a Madhouse & quite forget your Name or who you are you must excuse me for I have nothing to com-mu[n]icate or tell of & why I am shut up I dont know I have nothing to say so I conclude   *yours respectfully*

JOHN CLARE

But these are exceptional moments. Though I could tell you the story of my life, if that were my purpose, simply by describing its mail, I suppose what matters most are the links, the dull ordinary passage of days, the communiqués that go back and forth with common sense and regularity and on which we come to depend and take for granted like sunlight itself. Until one day you receive on your doorstep all the letters you wrote the deceased.

When someone dies, it is standard decorum to return to those who wrote them the letters found in the possession of the deceased. If the senders are themselves deceased, it is standard decorum to burn the letters—not to rip them up or put them in the trash, but to burn them. You'd be surprised how many people are unaware of this. Just how faithfully these procedures are followed has altered the course of the history of history that we call scholarship.

Insert here hundreds of examples.

> Susie, what shall I do—there is'nt room enough; not *half* enough, to hold what I was going to say. Wont you tell the man who makes sheets of paper, that I hav'nt the *slightest respect* for him!

EMILY DICKINSON

The extant, vital, fresh, ongoing exchanges we make in this life, if we are writers, afford us other opportunities to be writers. In other words, the noncorporeal mind-voice, in a forum free of the disservices of the public, allows us to extend the same grace and possibility we so desperately seek in our poems. Many will disagree, but for me, I do not care if I am writing a poem or a letter—it is just making marks on a sheet of paper that delights and envelops me. What I am trying to tell you is this: every time you write an unengaged letter, you are wasting another opportunity to be a writer. The greater the disparity between the voice of your poems and the voice of your letters, the greater the circumference of the point you have missed. The demands upon you, as a writer, are far greater than you could have guessed when you filled out your application form and mailed it. How far are you willing to travel this love you profess to have for words?

To recipient unknown   *about 1861*

Master.

If you saw a bullet hit a Bird—and he told you he was'nt shot—you might weep at his courtesy, but you would certainly doubt his word.

One drop more from the gash that stains your Daisy's bosom—then would you believe? Thomas' faith in Anatomy, was stronger than his faith in faith. God made me— [Sir] Master—I did'nt be—myself. I dont know how it was done. He built the heart in me—Bye and bye it outgrew me—and like the little mother—with the big child—I got tired holding him. I heard of a thing called "Redemption" —which rested men and women. You remember I asked you for it—you gave me something else. I forgot the Redemption [in the Redeemed—I did'nt tell you for a long time, but I knew you had altered me—I] and was tired—no more—[so dear did this stranger become that were it, or my breath—the Alternative—I had tossed the fellow away with a smile.] I am older—tonight, Master—but the love is the same—so are the moon and the crescent. If it had been

God's will that I might breathe where you breathed—and find the place—myself—at night—if I (can) never forget that I am not with you—and that sorrow and frost are nearer than I—if I wish with a might I cannot repress—that mine were the Queen's place—the love of the Plantagenet is my only apology—To come nearer than presbyteries—and nearer than the new Coat—that the Tailor made—the prank of the Heart at play on the Heart—in holy Holiday—is forbidden me—You make me say it over—I fear you laugh—when I do not see—[but] "Chillon" is not funny. Have you the Heart in your breast—Sir—is it set like mine—a little to the left—has it the misgiving—if it wake in the night—perchance—itself to it—a timbrel is it—itself to it a tune?

These things are [reverent] holy, Sir, I touch them [reverently] hallowed, but persons who pray—dare remark [our] "Father"! You say I do not tell you all—Daisy confessed—and denied not.

Vesuvius dont talk—Etna—dont—[Thy] one of them—said a syllable—a thousand years ago, and Pompeii heard it, and hid forever—She could'nt look the world in the face, afterward—I suppose—Bashfull Pompeii! "Tell you of the want"—you know what a leech is, dont you—and [remember that] Daisy's arm is small—and you have felt the horizon hav'nt you—and did the sea—never come so close as to make you dance?

I dont know what you can do for it—thank you—Master

213

—but if I had the Beard on my cheek—like you—and you—had Daisy's petals—and you cared so for me—what would become of you? Could you forget me in fight, or flight—or the foreign land? Could'nt Carlo, and you and I walk in the meadows an hour—and nobody care but the Bobolink—and his—a silver scruple? I used to think when I died—I could see you—so I died as fast as I could—but the "Corporation" are going Heaven too so [Eternity] wont be sequestered—now [at all]—Say I may wait for you—say I need go with no stranger to the to me—untried [country] fold—I waited a long time—Master—but I can wait more—wait till my hazel hair is dappled—and you carry the cane—then I can look at my watch—and if the Day is too far declined—we can take the chances [of] for Heaven—What would you do with me if I came "in white?" Have you the little chest to put the Alive—in?

I want to see you more—Sir—than all I wish for in this world—and the wish—altered a little—will be my only one —for the skies.

Could you come to New England—[this summer—could] would you come to Amherst—Would you like to come—Master?

[Would it do harm—yet we both fear God—] Would Daisy disappoint you—no—she would'nt—Sir—it were comfort forever—just to look in your face, while you looked in mine—then I could play in the woods till Dark—till you take me where Sundown cannot find us—and the true keep coming—till the town is full. [Will you tell me if you will?]

I did'nt think to tell you, you did'nt come to me "in white," nor ever told me why,

No Rose, yet felt myself a'bloom,

No Bird—yet rode in Ether.

Nobody wants his grave spray-painted and then vomited on, but these things happen to Jim Morrison's grave in Paris, and those who do it maintain they are not being disrespectful, or dishonoring his memory; they are being sincere in their homage and tribute. It would make an interesting trial, ethically speaking.

Irreverence and sincerity are not opposed; we all know this, yet it is a common occurrence in life that our behavior is in direct opposition to what we know.

Both the irreverent and the sincere congratulate themselves and they have the sin of pride in common. Both can be feigned, and both depend on the eye of the beholder.

Irreverence implies a word or act that strips a person or thing of its dignity, but a subversive word or act that is irreverent on the surface may be an attempt to *restore* a dignity or autonomy that has been lost to those in the margins.

No one truly irreverent—bent on defaming the dignity of the genre—would take the time to be a poet, for the simple reason it takes so much time, and I have often observed that people usually spend their time doing what they like to do.

Irreverence is a way of playing hooky and remaining present at the same time.

Irreverence and sincerity are both forms of exaggeration, yet Gauguin maintained there is no such thing as exaggerated art— he, of course, did not have to speak as he painted. His medium was not under constant scrutiny by everyday users of its particles.

The truth on the page does not distinguish between the lived and unlived, the irreverent, the sincere, the eggplant and aubergine. You can't be Job when you read, you have to be God.

When T. S. Eliot and Groucho Marx met, Groucho wanted to discuss *The Waste Land* and Eliot wanted to discuss *Duck Soup*.

All subjects are the same; we're wondering if life has any meaning at all outside the sensory pleasures of being alive that are briefly granted to most (but not all) of us.

Isn't all art irreverent? It is irreverent to create that which doesn't exist; the newly made thing flies in the face of the already created and as such is based on negation (what already exists is simply not enough!), but born also out of the greatest reverence for all that already is. When Borges, visiting the Sahara, picked up a little bit of sand, carried it in his hand and let it fall someplace else, he said, "I am modifying the Sahara," and he wrote that this was one of the most significant memories of his stay. What Borges did is what we do when we write poems after millennia of poem writing. We aren't saving the Sahara, we are modifying it, and you have to be irreverent to think you can modify the Sahara in the first place, and sincere in your attempt to do so.

Art is irreverent in another way: it can shatter fixed ideas; how can the "sudden growth" (Pound's term) it engenders take place unless something is shattered?

The poem, more than any other art form in existence, is the perfect vehicle for the direct expression of personal love. I think this is why, given the long history of love utterances in poetry, most people equate and continue to equate poetry with unqualified sincerity that has somehow escaped the mouth. The poem as a made thing, the poem as imaginative vision, as a moment of *searching*—all this is secondary to most people's desire and demand for an understandable truth that will make them happy. And who can blame them? It's heartbreaking.

Mostly we've been educated to perceive irreverence and sincerity. We've been educated in our responses, and it has been helpful and even necessary, but one reaches the point—if one is to continue to make or behold art—where such assumptions no longer facilitate the personality who seeks to remain vulnerable to the unknown.

I read an interview with Margaret Mead in which she said, surprisingly, that declarative sentences are not important, they are merely incidental statements. "If one goes into a strange society and can do these three things, ask a question accurately, give a command accurately, and gloom and exclaim and enthuse at the proper moments, most of the rest of what you have to do is listen." I don't know anything about anthropology or linguistics, but it sure reminded me of poetry.

If there were a perfume named Sincerity and a perfume named Irreverence, I'd choose Irreverence, on the assumption the top and base notes would be somewhat contradictory. But in a line of lipsticks, I'd choose Sincerity, based on sentiment and hoping for a pure, deep color . . . my own impulses are therefore confused: my lips sincere and my gestures irreverent.

I offer my dinner guest, after dinner, the choice between regular and decaf coffee, when in fact I don't have any decaf in the house. I am so sincere in my effort to be a good host that I lie; I think this probably happens all the time in poetry.

You hear so much talk about risk-taking in poetry. Lying is a form of risk-taking, but no one talks about that.

If there is any irreverence in my own work, I hope it is the irreverence I bear in mistrusting my own sincere self, which then sincerely mistrusts the irreverent me. If there is a bottom to this, I think it is a life's work.

There really *is* a beach in Western Australia where kangaroos swim in the sea and sunbathe afterward, those short white forelegs stretched in the sand.

Nothing would make me happier than to see an international ban on fact-checking.

Was Walt Whitman irreverent or sincere when he wrote his first unrhymed poem (March 22, 1850)?

"How often we forget that to stimulate and to satisfy oppose each other!" Paul Valéry.

James Wright announcing he is speaking in a flat voice, then quoting the King James Bible.

Emerson: "To believe your own thought, to believe that what is true for you in your private heart is true for all men—that is genius." One of the more radical statements ever made, and if true, it would have to be true whether the private thoughts were sincere or irreverent.

After he was decapitated, Saint Denis walked with his head in his hands . . . an act of irreverence toward those who had beheaded him, an act of sincerity toward his own self's faith.

Irreverence usually hides an unnatural obsession with what is revered. He who doubts wants to be believed, he who hides wants to be found. He who curses with regularity uses God's name as often as one who prays.

Youth versus age. Play versus work.

Most artistic "movements" will be irreverent toward whatever movement preceded theirs. In that sense, almost all movements are adolescent—absolutely necessary and inevitable and their manifestos ridiculous.

Remember also that the "youth culture" of this country, founded after the Second World War, is an enormous economic force, a commodity unto itself. If it is based on irreverence, that irreverence continues to make money, unabated. Revolt has the capacity to grow very rich very fast.

Some poets are sincere in their youth and irreverent in old age (Yeats) while others are irreverent in their youth and sincere in old age (Wordsworth).

A poem is a finished work of the mind, it is not the work of a finished mind.

What about Neil Armstrong, who wishes he could go back up there and take his footsteps away?

All the major religions in the world have sects that employ irreverence as a valuable tool for transmitting theology.

"There is such a thing as sincerity. It is hard to define but it is probably nothing but your highest liveliness escaping from a succession of dead selves. Miraculously. It is the same with illusions. Any belief you sink into when you should be leaving it behind is an illusion." Robert Frost.

If seeing something beautiful "de-centers" you, as Simone Weil maintains, and is conducive to goodness, I can't disagree, I can only add that seeing something irreverent toward that beauty—a carcass as opposed to a rose, Mona Lisa with a beard as opposed to without—also has the power to de-center you, and it is also conducive to goodness. They don't show those cadavers to the monks for nothing!

If irreverence is audacity, then the most irreverent poem in existence must be "This Living Hand" by John Keats. It is absolutely appropriate that it was written as marginalia; for the marginalized, the excluded, the unrepresented and unrepresentable, are desperately unhappy, and irreverence is born in unhappy soil.

I am a great believer in mood as the final arbiter of perception. What you like in October won't necessarily hold any appeal in January. I think this is particularly true of poetry: X, whom you read with relish in October, might be a bloody bore in January. It happens. But to have a poet bring you out of one mood and into another—that's the most powerful experience of all.

To those who think poetry is dependent on the past: it isn't. It is dependent on the present, the moment of the poem's making, the mysterious presence of its absence (that pressure in the head), and after the artifact of the poem has been made it becomes, rather quickly, a thing of the past, and so readers and critics will treat it as a past event—the one thing the poem was unaware of, and didn't want to be—and yet became, was becoming! If poetry was dependent on the past, there would be no such thing as young poets, and thank god there are and thank god they stupefy us.

You cannot eradicate personal experience: you cannot. You can destroy people, you can kill whole populations, but you cannot destroy the sense of personal existence that the living still carry as they are borne forward in time. When I think of life, I think of my own personal existence as it is borne forward in time, or I think of the lives of billions of strangers as they are being borne forward in time, but I seldom think of myself and these billions at once. It is the difference between Life and being alive. I do not know on which day I am most being sincere. And then there are those days I think only of the dead, and those are the days I think of everybody together—myself, the strangers, the dead—because we are all of a group, we are a class unto ourselves. To consider myself and others among the already-dead, is that irreverent of me?

You simply cannot learn and know at the same time, and this is a frustration all artists must bear.

"Two tasks at the beginning of your life: to narrow your orbit more and more, and ever and again to check whether you are not in hiding somewhere outside your orbit." Franz Kafka.

I REMEMBER, I REMEMBER

I remember being so young I thought all artists were famous.

I remember being so young I thought all artists were good, kind, loving, exceptionally interesting, and exemplary human beings.

I remember—I must have been eight or nine—wandering out to the ungrassed backyard of our newly constructed suburban house, and seeing that the earth was dry and cracked in irregular squares and other shapes and I felt I was *looking at a map* and I was completely overcome by this description, my first experience of making a metaphor, and I felt weird and shaky and went inside and wrote it down: the cracked earth is a map. Although it only takes a little time to tell it, and it is hardly interesting, it filled a big moment at the time, it was an enormous ever-expanding room of a moment, a chunk of time that has expanded ever since and that my whole life keeps fitting into.

I remember writing a letter to President John F. Kennedy and a few weeks after mailing it finding it in the bottom of my mother's drawer.

I remember sending my poems to Little, Brown and Company, and suggesting they title the collection "The Little Golden Book of Verse," and I remember their rejection was very kind and I was stunned when they made a guess at my age and were correct, I *was* in the fourth grade, and I felt the people at Little, Brown and Company were so smart they could read minds.

I remember I chose Little, Brown and Company for a very special reason: they were the publishers of my favorite author, Laura Ingalls Wilder, who wrote the *Little House on the Prairie* books (this was long before the television series). And although Little, Brown and Company sent me a very kind letter indeed, and guessed my age, they also did something I could never forgive them for, something that upset me for days and weeks and months. They sent me a picture of Laura Ingalls Wilder as a ninety-year-old woman; they told me she was dead, her mother and father and sisters were all dead too, and her husband, and that one of my favorite characters had died in a threshing machine accident—*a threshing machine accident*—it was so specific I was able to picture it vividly in my imagination, the mangled body in its overalls, the hat fallen off, some blood on the ground, the machine stopped in the noonday sun, one of its wheels bent out of shape, or some spoke or cog, and a leg or arm was in there, and the whole scene took place in the center of miles and miles and miles—as far as you could see— of beautiful golden grain, all the same length, like a crew cut.

I remember I was not exactly sure what a threshing machine was.

I remember they said that although Pa was dead, his fiddle was in a museum somewhere, and once a year somebody took it out of its case and played it. I remember feeling sorry for the violin, and thinking how lonely it must be to live like that, in a museum.

I remember when I was in the fifth grade my grandfather died and it was my first funeral and when everyone was filing out of the funeral parlor I remember asking if Grandpap was going to stay in there all alone at night and they said yes and I thought that would be awfully scary, lying in a coffin in an empty building, just like the fiddle in its case.

I remember when I was forty-five and my mother died it poured the day we buried her and late at night I thought of how cold her body must be, with the freezing rain pouring down on it, and how much she would hate being out in the cold and rain if she were alive. She would want to be under the blankets of her own bed on such a night, with a cup of coffee on the nightstand, and the coffee would be on top of the first art object I ever made, at the age of five, a ceramic coaster: a white tile with my face drawn on it in brown lines. For forty years her coffee cup must have burned my face, and since my mother died by fire, I did not want to think of it anymore.

"I remember, I remember, / The house where I was born" are the first two lines of a famous poem called "I Remember, I Remember" by a not-so-famous poet named Thomas Hood, and it was in the first poetry book I ever owned, *The Golden Treasury of Poetry*, edited by Louis Untermeyer.

I remember (later) thinking it was a curious thing, that there were so many famous poems by not-so-famous poets.

I remember (later) being shocked when I discovered Hood was a contemporary of Keats, only four years younger; I always thought of him as a later Victorian, for the diction of the two poets is remarkably different. No matter how you look at this, the implications are truly startling: either the lesser Hood was ahead of his time, or the greater Keats (Miltonian) was behind his time. It means poetry is more than the sum of its diction.

I remember I recognized the allusion when I read Philip Larkin's version of "I Remember, I Remember." Larkin's poem is also called "I Remember, I Remember," and in it his train happens to stop in Coventry and he happens to remember he was born there. The last line of the poem is "Nothing, like something, happens anywhere."

I remember my Thanksgiving poem being pinned to the school bulletin board, where everyone could see it, and leaves cut out of orange construction paper were stapled all around it. It is the one poem I am still trying to write.

I remember in high school there was a girl named Lizette. She had black hair and a very pale face and because her mother was French she was an outsider and to make matters worse she was not the best student but was awfully good at art and took all the art classes and we worked on the literary magazine together and I liked her very much but I was afraid to be her friend because after all she was strange and I think I was jealous of her strangeness at the same time as I was afraid of it, and when we were together we read our poems out loud to each other, and in this way, through poetry, it was always safe to communicate.

I remember (much later) wondering what ever happened to Lizette.

I remember another friend in high school whose mother was an artist and their house was full of statues—the Buddha and nymphs—and the furniture looked like it was hundreds of years old and there were paintings on the wall and her mother had a separate apartment called a studio and in it were figures of clay on pedestals and in one corner an old hand-cranked gramophone and I liked being in there but it was kinda scary too, it seemed forbidden in some way I couldn't figure out; art was scary, strange, forbidden and the really confusing part was I wanted it and needed it.

I remember one afternoon my friend and I were in the studio and all the clay figures on pedestals were draped with white sheets and my friend told me her mother did that when she didn't want to look at them anymore and I was totally confused.

I remember standing in a field in Switzerland at dusk, surrounded by cows with bells around their necks, and reading John Keats's "Ode to a Nightingale" out loud from an open book I was holding in my hands, and I started to weep—*weep* is a better word for it than *cry*—and I remember the tears slowly streaming down my face, it was that beautiful to me, and I loved poetry that much. I was eighteen.

I remember (later) thinking that it was actually hilarious that I used to read poetry to cows, that they were an integral part of my most serious moment.

I remember in junior high my leg was in a cast and it was summer and I was lying on a sofa in the basement where it was cool; there was a TV down there, and an ironing board, and a room for my sister to stay in when she came home from college, and my sister was ironing—she was always ironing, sewing, or cooking, she was majoring in Home Economics—and to pass the time she gave me one of her college textbooks, a book of poems by the British Romantics, and the only other thing I can remember is that my life changed that summer. My life changed for good.

I remember when I graduated from college, we were asked to submit exactly how we wanted our names to appear on our diplomas, and I spelled my middle name (which is Lorraine) Low Rain, because the day before I had been reading W. S. Merwin's new book and in it was some kind of brief Japanese thing along the lines of "Low Rain, Roof Fell."

I remember when my parents saw my diploma, they were horrified and kept asking me how I could have done such a thing, after they paid for my education and all.

I remember finding the diploma among my mother's things after she died, and throwing it away.

I remember I never did like to save things much.

I remember saving everything.

I remember the afternoon I sat in a literature class, my hardback edition of *The Collected Poems of Wallace Stevens* open before me, a book I had already owned for years, the pages worn and softened by endless turning and fingering, page after page filled with marginalia, notes, the definitions of words, question marks, exclamation marks, and underlinings, all in the soft gray graphite of my own living penciling hand, when a distracted classmate I did not know very well leaned over my book and wrote in it with her ballpoint pen: *I'm so bored!!! Are you going to the party tonight?* I remember feeling like my blood had stopped and reversed course, not in the heart, where that is supposed to happen, but midvein, the feeling medically called *shock*. I remember trembling and soaring with anger, and I remember the weekend after the unfortunate incident took place, sitting for hours and hours in my room with a new book, trying to cope, copying by hand everything I had ever written in the old book, with the exception of that one bold, sorry, uninvited guest.

I remember, in college, trying to write a poem while I was stoned, and thinking it was the best thing I had ever written.

I remember reading it in the morning, and throwing it out.

I remember thinking, If W. S. Merwin could do it, why couldn't I?

I remember thinking, Because he is a god and I am a hand-maiden with a broken urn.

I remember the first poetry reading I ever went to; I was in college and it was W.S. Merwin. He sat on a stool under a spotlight and the audience sat at his feet. He had a halo of curls and he looked like a god with his face in the spotlight. He wore blue velvet knee breeches, a flowing white shirt, and soft, flat yellow leather boots—more like slippers really—that came up to his knees, where his trousers began. Surely this is an imaginary memory, surely he never owned such clothing.

I remember liking the reading.

I remember being young and liking everything.

I remember liking a great many readings that, if I were to sit through them now, I would not like.

I remember hearing the great Spanish poet Rafael Alberti read. I was very young and so he seemed very old to me, with his shoulder-length white hair and his white suit. I was also shocked that he was accompanied by a woman who did not seem to be much older than I was; she wore a skirt so short you could see her underwear when she walked, and white plastic go-go boots, as they were called. I remember one of them carried a birdcage with a white dove in it, but to tell the truth I may have made this detail up, in my mind over the years, perhaps to emphasize to myself that it was, and remains, the strangest poetry reading I ever attended. Alberti read his poems in Spanish and his American translator, Ben Belitt, read them in English. Ben was sober, shy, outwardly conservative; he wore a tweed jacket and tie. Alberti gave Ben a toy pistol, what was called a cap gun, a toy capable of making very loud noises, and told Ben to shoot himself in the head whenever he, Alberti, gave the signal, and that is exactly what happened: Alberti would be reading in Spanish, pause, look at Ben, and Ben would reluctantly shoot himself in the head. But when Ben read the poems in English, Alberti had the pistol and from time to time shot himself in the head with real gusto. I felt it was a great lesson in translation.

I remember hearing James Merrill read, in August, in Vermont, in a barn. He wore a white linen suit and read to a very small group of people (no more than twenty) sitting on folding metal chairs; I remember a shaft of light coming in through an open window and that I spent most of the reading watching the dust motes floating there. Beyond that—nothing, except one detail, the memory of which overrides all else: outside, a car was parked (had he arrived in it?), its rear window was filthy, and someone has written in the dust *clean me*, in Greek. I always instinctively knew he had written it, and that rear window is my memory of James Merrill.

I remember my first Ashbery reading, also in college. Ashbery was reading from his new book, *Three Poems*, and he said that it was a lot like watching TV—you could open the book anywhere and begin reading, and flip around the book as much as you wanted to. I remember hating him for saying this. I remember the word *sacrilege* came to mind. I remember not liking that reading.

I remember, two years later, reading *Three Poems* on a grassy slope while across the road three men put a new roof on an old house, and I was in love with one of them. I could watch the men working as I read. I remember that everything I was reading was everything that was happening across the way—I would read a little, then look up, read a little, then look up, and I was blown apart by the feeling this little book was about my life at that moment, exactly as I was living it. I remember loving

the book, and that it was one of the memorable reading expe-
riences of my life.

I remember reading Rilke's Duino Elegies again and again and
again, until I "got" them, until something burst over me like a
flood, and I remember, once again, weeping and weeping with
a book in my hands.

I remember a reading W. S. Merwin gave in a tiny chapel, with
the audience sitting in the pews, and how after a while we were
all lost in a suspension of time—I know I was—and after the
reading there was a Q&A and someone asked a bizarre ques-
tion, she asked what time it was, and Merwin looked at the
clock (there was a clock on the wall) and every one of us could
see it had stopped, it had stopped in the middle of his reading,
literal proof of what we already felt to be true, this spectacular
thing, the dream of all poetry, to cut a hole in time.

I remember wanting to hear Anne Carson read, but I was very
ill and had to be admitted to the hospital, and I postponed my
going into the hospital until the next morning, after I had heard
her read. I remember I needed a ride to the hospital but none
of my friends could take me, they wouldn't take me, because
there were a lot of famous poets in town, and they wanted to
hear them all. I remember this made me angry beyond words,

but at the same time it was hypocritical of me, because I myself had put off my hospitalization until after a reading.

I remember the year after college I was broke, and Bernard Malamud, who had been a teacher of mine, sent me a check for $25 and told me to buy food with it, and I went downtown and bought *The Collected Poems of W. B. Yeats.*

I remember John Moore, another teacher, who did the damnedest thing. We were studying Yeats, and at the beginning of one class Mr. Moore asked us if we would like to see a picture of Yeats. We nodded, and he held up a photograph of Yeats taken when he was six months old, a baby dressed in a long white gown. Maybe he was even younger, maybe he was an infant. I thought it was the funniest thing anyone had ever done, the strangest, most ridiculous, absurd thing to have done. But nobody laughed and if Mr. Moore thought it was funny, you couldn't tell by his face. I always liked him for that. The poems we were reading in class were not written by a baby. And yet whenever I think of Yeats, I see him as a tiny baby wearing a dress—that photograph is part of my conception of the great Irish poet. And I love that it is so. We are all so small.

I remember going to New York for an awards ceremony, for I had won an award, and standing awkwardly in a grand lobby, and noticing an old man in a white hat who looked rather lost, and thinking he had come to see someone get an award, perhaps a granddaughter or someone like that, and I went up to him and asked him if I could help him, and he asked me where the men's room was, and I walked him there, and while we were walking I asked him if perhaps a member of his family was receiving an award, and he said not that he knew of, and then he went into the bathroom and I waited for him outside and while I was waiting I remember thinking how surprised he would be when he found out that I, the woman who showed him the bathroom, was receiving an award, and then a man and a woman walked by in an important kind of hurry, saying, "We have lost Arthur Miller," and then Mr. Miller came out of the bathroom, and smiled at me and shrugged his shoulders and went away with them.

I remember my first electric typewriter.

I remember sending my first short story out to a national magazine the summer after I had graduated from college, and receiving the reply, "We are terribly sorry, but we don't publish poetry." I remember never looking back.

I remember meeting an Irish poet who had just come from Georgie Yeats's funeral, and was still drunk, though he had also just flown from Ireland to the United States. He was furious and maudlin because Georgie, who outlived her husband by

thirty years, died only weeks after she had given all her hus-
band's manuscripts to the Irish State, manuscripts she could
have sold to an American university for millions of dollars; she
did this because she had no money, was an alcoholic, and very
much afraid in a moment of weakness she would break down
and sell the manuscripts after all; the thought of such a betrayal
she could not bear, so she gave the papers to the Irish State,
died a few weeks later, and had a three-hundred-mile funeral
cortege with only six people present—the poet who told me
this was one of them—and not a single representative of the
Irish State was among them.

I remember another thing the Irish poet told me: Once, drink-
ing in Dublin with Berryman, they had a shot of ouzo and
Berryman immediately disappeared. It was a matter of hours
before they discovered he had walked out of the bar, taken a
taxi to the airport and flown directly to Athens using his Amer-
ican Express card.

I remember reading John Berryman's Dream Song #14 in my
twenties, with its famous opening words, "Life, friends, is bor-
ing." I remember being struck by its wit, irony, playfulness, de-
light: it is the kind of poem students read aloud to each other
in a pool of laughter and admiration, and there is nothing
wrong with that, for it reinforces their sense of cynicism and su-
periority, and it is crucial at that age we find a like-minded

group to whom we can belong. I remember rereading the poem, not for the second time, some thirty years later, and being struck by its excruciating pain, which is entirely without irony. Many persons who knew Berryman have remarked that he spoke, always, without irony, which means, simply, that he always meant what he said. If you are going through a particularly stable period of your life, and you encounter his bleakest statements, you will react with chagrin and disbelief, as if listening to the ablest jester. If you are going through a particularly unstable period of your life, the straightforward articulation of suffering that has already twisted and dislocated its bearer renders a tension that will very nearly kill you. But I did not know this then.

I remember reading in the newspaper that Ernest Hemingway was dead of a self-inflicted gunshot wound to the head, and reading the whole article to the end, which is a very strange memory, as I was ten years old and did not read the newspaper.

I remember figuring out Djuna Barnes was alive and living in Greenwich Village when I was in college and for a long time afterward, and I could have gone and visited her, but I assumed the author of my most beloved book had died before I was born.

I remember repeating this mistake for many years.

I remember making it yesterday.

I remember that Djuna Barnes was living in total obscurity that last decade of her life, and so was I—if we can extend the meaning of the word *obscurity* to include a state of nonalert mind.

I remember that I did not always know authors were ordinary people living ordinary lives, and that an ordinary life was an obscure life, if we can extend the meaning of *obscure* to mean covered up by dailiness, glorious dailiness, shameful dailiness, dailiness that is difficult to figure out, that is not always clear until a long time afterward. Obscure: not readily noticed, easily understood, or clearly expressed. Which is a pretty good definition of life.

I remember, I remember the house where I was born.

I remember driving by the hospital where I was born and glancing at it—I was in a car going sixty miles an hour—and feeling a fleeting twinge of specialness after which I had no choice but to let it go and get over it, at sixty miles an hour.

I remember I was a child, and when I grew up I was a poet. It all happened at sixty miles an hour and on days when the clock stopped and all of humanity fit into a little chapel, into a pinecone, a shot of ouzo, a snail's shell, a piece of soggy rye on the pavement.

I remember the day I stood in front of a great, famous sculpture by a great, famous sculptor and didn't like it. Such a moment is a landmark in the life of any young artist. It begins in confusion and guilt and self-doubt and ends in a triumphant break-through: I see the world and I see that I am free before it, I am not at the mercy of historical opinion and what I want to turn away from, I turn away from, what I want to approach, I approach. Twenty-five years later I read an essay by John Berger on Rodin and in it Berger was able to articulate all that I felt on that afternoon, standing in front of a great Rodin. But by then I was old and vain and the pride of being vindicated was, I admit, just as exciting as Berger's intellectual condemnation of Rodin's desire toward dominance.

I remember thinking my feelings implicated me with Rodin and though now I liked him less than ever, my repulsion was braided with a profound sympathy inseparable from my feelings for myself. And that is a landmark in the life of an old artist looking at art: the realization that none of us can ever be free from ourselves.

I remember the first time I realized the world we are born into is not the one we leave.

I remember feeling my head was made of sandpaper.

I remember feeling my head was made of the smoothest silver driftwood.

I remember Ben Belitt, Pablo Neruda's friend and translator, bent down to pick up the *New York Times* from his doorstoop one rainy morning (this was before they had figured out you could put the newspaper in a plastic sleeve) and the first thing he noticed was that the "newspaper had been crying," as he put it, that the newsprint was smudged and ran together in watery lines down the page, just like mascara, and then he saw the announcement of Neruda's death: Neruda had died the night before.

I remember telling this story many times, but leaving Ben out of it, pretending it was me it had happened to.

I remember the night I decided I would call myself a poet. I had been invited to a dinner party of literati, and I knew I would inevitably be asked what I did. I usually said I was a teacher; I was twenty-seven years old and had been writing poems since I was nine. I made up my mind that if anyone asked, I would say I was a poet; I left my apartment with resolve, a sense of mission, and security. And someone asked. Alain, a charismatic French poet wearing a blue velvet jacket and a long white scarf, asked me what I did; I took a deep breath and said I was a poet; his face distorted into a human field of disgust: "A poet!" he cried. "If you call yourself a poet then you cannot possibly be one; poets live in shadows and never admit and do not discuss, and besides, a real poet knows that all the poems in the world do not a poet make. I would no more call myself a poet than call myself a man—it is the height of arrogance, as any dog knows." Dear me! I left the party in tears—hard cold tears of confusion and humiliation. It seemed my final hour.

I remember, I remember, everything you said to me. We went walking out in silence, underneath the cherry tree. Falling blossom, falling blossom, falling from the cherry tree. I remember, I remember, everything you did to me: Annie Lennox, "Twisted." There, the famous refrain from English poetry finds its way into rock and roll, more than a hundred years later.

I remember "remember" means to put the arms and legs back on, and sometimes the head.

I remember, on the first Tuesday of every year, that I became a poet for a single, simple reason: I liked making similes for the moon. And when things get tough and complicated and threaten to drown me in their innuendoes, I come back to this clear, simple, and elemental fact, out of all facts the one most like the moon itself. *O night, sleep, death and the stars!*

I remember the moon was covered with dust and I used my finger to write *clean me* on its surface, and my finger was ever after covered with a fine gray blanket, as when you pull lint from the dryer.

I remember more than I can tell.

I remember heaven.

I remember hell.

TWENTY-TWO SHORT LECTURES

WHY ALL OUR LITERARY
PURSUITS ARE USELESS

Eighty-five percent of all existing species are beetles and various forms of insects.

English is spoken by only 5 percent of the world's population.

WHY THERE MAY BE HOPE

One of the greatest stories ever written is the story of a man
who wakes to find himself transformed into a giant beetle.

SHORT LECTURE ON SHAKESPEARE

They say there are no known facts about Shakespeare, because if it were his pen name, as many believe, then whom that bed was willed to is a moot point. Yet there is one hard cold clear fact about him, a fact that freezes the mind that dares to contemplate it: in the beginning William Shakespeare was a baby, and knew absolutely nothing. He couldn't even speak.

SHORT LECTURE ON SOCRATES

I am forever telling my students I know nothing about poetry, and they never believe me. I do not know what my poems are about, except on rare occasions, and I never know what they mean. I have met and spoken to many poets who feel the same way, and one among them once put it this way: "The difference between myself and a student is that I am better at not knowing what I am doing." I couldn't put it any better than that if I tried.

But consider this: when someone admits they know nothing, their words go back to the very beginnings of Western civilization, Hellas, Attica, Greece, a civilization you may not give a fig about, but one that flourished and existed, for better and for worse, and one that continues to shape and influence the country you are living in today. The foundations of this ancient civilization rise up and hover beneath anyone who says they know nothing, for those words belong to Socrates, the teacher of

Plato, Plato, his student, being the distillation of Western civilization in a single human body.

Socrates said the only true wisdom consists in knowing that you know nothing. It is his basic premise, one from which all his other thoughts come. And here is the story behind it: The oracle at Delphi, a shrine of prophecy, said that no man living was wiser than Socrates. Socrates was a philosopher and wanted to test the statement in order to prove it true or false. First he went to the politicians—this was in Athens, the first democracy in the Western world, around 430 BC (albeit one that excluded slaves and women); well, he went to the politicians because they had been elected, presumably, on the merit of their wisdom; Socrates soon found out they knew nothing, but thought they knew everything. He said he supposed therefore he was wiser than they were, since at least he knew he knew nothing. Then he went to the poets, to see how wise they were, for there were many wise things in their writings, and the people marveled over them, and among the poets he discovered an interesting thing (interesting to us, that is, since we are poets); he found out that the poets did not compose out of wisdom, but out of inspiration, and they were more like prophets who said many fine things but did not themselves understand any of it. But the poets thought they were wise, on account of all their poetry. So he nixed them, too. Then Socrates went to the craftsmen, the men who made boats and sandals and pots (keep in mind that today we believe poets to be craftsmen, too), and he found that indeed they knew many things about making boats and sandals and pots, and upon this knowledge assumed they were wise, but in reality their wisdom was directly tied to the specific skill they possessed, and could not be carried outside it. And so Socrates concluded that what the oracle at Delphi meant was not that Socrates was wise but that at least he knew he knew nothing.

Now I have told you something about Socrates, and I suspect I have made you very happy, for a moment ago you knew nothing, and now you know something.

SHORT LECTURE ON THE DEAD

I never believed, for a moment, that anyone ever learned a single thing about poetry from hearing a lecture. Don't misunderstand me; lectures are important insofar as they teach us how to *talk* about poems, but never do they teach us how to write them. Nothing does. Except, sometimes, the dead. Why is that, I wondered, when poetry is alive and well insofar as plenty of still-beating hearts are writing it? And I came to believe—call me delusional—that no living poet, none, could teach us a single thing about poetry for the simple fact that no living poet has a clue as to what he or she is doing, at least none I have talked to, and I have talked to quite a few. John Ashbery and Billy Collins can't teach you a thing, for the simple fact that they are living. Why is that, I wondered. I mean I really wondered. I think it is because poets are people—no matter what camp they sleep in—who are obsessed with the one thing no one knows anything about. That would be death. They talk to the dead and have a rapport with the dead and write about death as if they had done it, which is utterly ridiculous because they are not dead and never have been and cannot teach us a single thing about death and being dead. And yet—here's the weird thing—THE MINUTE THEY BECOME DEAD THEY CAN TEACH US EVERYTHING. Why, why is that? I think it's because the minute they are dead all of their poems about death become poems about being alive. And we are alive and can be taught something about that. I mean it. John Ashbery or Billy Collins can teach you nothing about poetry today, July 21, 2009, but if one of them were to die tomorrow he could teach you something about poetry on July 23, 2009. *Poets are dead people talking about being alive.* It's that simple. People who are alive are not really people because they haven't died; but people who have been alive and then died are the whole kind of people we want to be our teachers. I really can't explain it, being alive and all.

SHORT LECTURE IN THE FORM
OF A COURSE DESCRIPTION

My idea for a class is you just sit in the classroom and read aloud until everyone is smiling, and then you look around, and if someone is not smiling you ask them why, and then you keep reading—it may take many different books—until they start smiling, too.

SHORT LECTURE ON PRAYER

James Fenton, in *An Introduction to English Poetry*, puts forth
the idea that poetry happens when one raises their voice. I
agree, but I also believe that poetry happens when one lowers
their voice. In the first instance, the raised voice, we have the
street hawkers, the singers, the storytellers, the priests—any-
one who wants to be heard over the din—but in the second we
include the tellers of secrets, the lovers, the password keep-
ers—all those who want to be heard *beneath the din*, not by the
din itself but by one singular other who is part of the din, as
when in the middle of a concert we lean to the person next to
us and cup our hand around our mouth, forming a private am-
phitheater, a concert within a concert, connecting ourselves to
one the way the concert is connecting itself to everyone. And I
was thinking about prayer, and those who must raise their voice
in order to be heard in their emergency and desperation—*O
lord out of all those who are vying for your attention at this mo-*

ment please hear my prayer—and I think actually those raised prayers are directed toward the *gods*, in the plural sense, which would be a din, the din of gods, caretakers of all the multiple things that can happen to us. But the prayer of the lowered register no longer has a chance of being heard, has abandoned that chance—"given up," we say—yet retains the desire to speak, and I think these are the prayers addressed to *god*, who has become a *singular absence*: there is no one in the next seat; the ether becomes an ear.

Cries and whispers. A bang or a whimper. Whatever the case, if we want to be heard, we must raise our voice, or lower it.

SHORT LECTURE ON
YOUR OWN HAPPINESS

You know how to write poetry, it is all you need to be happy, but you will not be happy, you will be miserable, thinking you need so many other things, and in years and years of misery you have only one thing, as poets, to look forward to, the day you will not want what you haven't got, the thing you have got is poetry, let nothing cheat, steal, or deflect you from it, even poetry itself. Why are you sitting there? You should have fled before I finished the first sentence.

SHORT LECTURE ON VOICE

Hello.
Hi!
Hail to thee, blithe Spirit!
Out of the murderous innocence of the sea.
Nite-nite.

When students are searching for their voice, they are searching for poetry. When they find their voice, they will have found poetry. When they find poetry, they will live to regret it.

SHORT LECTURE ON
THE NATURE OF THINGS

(Turn vase into a hat and wear it)

You think the vase has become a hat; it has not.
My body has become an upside-down flower.

SHORT LECTURE ON TRANSLATION

I asked my friend the translator, What was the first known act of translation in the history of mankind? His answer was, Probably something into or out of Egyptian. I thought about this for a while and ventured a certainty: No, I said, it was when a mother heard her baby babble or cry, and had to decide in an instant what it meant.

SHORT LECTURE WRITTEN
BY A TEN-YEAR-OLD

Today at school I wrote an essay about Flag Day which was
so beautiful, but ever so beautiful—for I even used words
without really knowing what they meant.

CLARICE LISPECTOR, "Flying the Flag"

SHORT LECTURE ON HYPOCRISY

I despise people who talk on their cell phones while they are driving. When someone calls me I always ask if they are in their car and if they say yes I hang up. I have joined an organization whose sole purpose is to have cell phone usage in automobiles banned in each of the fifty states as soon as possible in one fell swoop (such bans are currently under state jurisdiction and not federally regulated, as they should be). I am a hypocrite. Every poem I have ever written has been written in my head while driving, the lines going round and round repeatedly in a loop of frenzied activity that does not stop until I reach a piece of paper; twice I have been stopped by authorities for traffic infractions I was unaware of: I could kill someone by writing a poem.

Every creative act is an act of hypocrisy and violence. You may have to think about it for a while, but I am sure you can discover your own.

SHORT LECTURE ON LYING

In this lecture I only lie three times. This is one of them.

SHORT LECTURE ENACTING
THE INNER LIFE OF A POET

(Play electronic man screaming "McKenna's lost his dog, Captain!" alternating with birdsong whistle)

SHORT LECTURE ON A PROBLEM

Every great poem has a problem, the problem of itself, and how it got stuck in space—how it got wedged in this world—the problem of being-in-the-first-place. This is not a problem one wants to eradicate; this is a problem one wants to preserve and honor, even as it eternally frustrates one, unsolvable as it is.

SHORT LECTURE ON EVOLUTION

The development of the human brain is a fascinating evolution. I mean the physical brain, the endless folding of the cerebrum and the cerebellum in such a small enclosed space as the human skull. All that folding is part of an attempt to include as many capacities and possibilities as possible inside the skull. The brain enfolded itself slowly, over millennia. A good question might be: Why didn't the brain just get bigger? Well, it did. It got bigger and the hip bones of women got bigger to accommodate the new size of the bigger brain in the bigger skull passing through the birth canal. Finally, though, simple enlargement reached the point where there would be skeletal instability if it went on much longer, and the species had to devise an alternative so the brain could keep growing. After all that endless folding came a time when the brain had to keep growing without there being any more space inside the skull: thus writing and reading evolved. Writing and reading are ways the brain can contain itself outside of itself. If you can't remember the ingredients you need to make dinner you make a list and voilá—a bit of your brain gets carried outside of itself. Eventually—more millennia—books came into being, and the human brain was able to keep expanding. A book is a physical expansion of the human brain. It is not an object to be treated lightly. When you hold a book in your hands you are holding a piece of cerebrum in your hands, like Saint Denis himself, who walked for miles carrying his head in his two hands, after he had been beheaded.

SHORT LECTURE ON THE BRAIN

Research on the human brain continues to be a "last frontier" of exploration; it is that and outer space—the two together representing the outer reaches of human seeking at this time. How we are to get along with each other remains, of course, the most crucial of the inner reaches, but as for the outer reaches—well friends, it's the brain and the stars.

So much research has been done, and reported on, that you and I are likely to take for granted certain conclusions that are bound to be knocked down and busted through and reduced to rubble in the future—and one of them has to do with creativity and has become, to my mind, such a cliché that we must be vigilant. I am talking about the right brain/left brain cliché.

The right hemisphere of the brain is the center of musical and artistic creation and the perception of shape and form, even the sense of humor. The left hemisphere generally controls the ability to read, speak, and do mathematical problems. This past semester I found myself, to my horror, telling a student to "write with your right brain and revise with your left."

But writers, clearly, have the ability to read and speak (left brain) and also the ability to understand shape and form, the fundamental aspects of artistic creation (right brain). I believe I myself possess both these abilities, and I do not jump back and forth between them; for me, they are the same thing; to write a sentence takes an understanding of form. I do not possess a shred of mathematical ability (left brain, the same side that enables me to read and write), nor do I possess a shred of musical ability (right brain, the same side that favors artistic creation). And it is a documented fact that many musicians are mathematically inclined, and many mathematicians musically inclined. And I don't think that a mathematician, at the end of the day, says to herself, "Time to give the left brain a rest, better pick up my violin."

The more I think about it, the stranger it becomes, because I do not think for an instant what you may be thinking now: *Oh Mary, it is a delicate balance and interplay between the two.* You see, I don't think there is anything balanced about artistic creation at all, I think it is a lopsided way of being, an obsessive and off-balance way of perceiving and being in the world; I mean, most people when they see a baby fox playing with butterflies don't have to write a poem about it, especially a poem where the baby fox winds up dead on the side of the road with butterflies gamboling around its splayed intestines.

But if artistic ability is connected to an understanding of shape and form, how can it be so off-balance in the first place? I mean, how can such off-balance people be so obsessed with shape and form?

How can the idea of balance reside at only one side of a seesaw?

This is what troubles me when I think about the notion of right brain/left brain. And every time I use the distinction, I am ashamed. Because I know it can't help an artist, nor can it help the person who can read and speak, and god help the one who is both.

SHORT LECTURE ON LECTURES

Ramakrishna said: Given a choice between going to heaven and hearing a lecture on heaven, people would choose a lecture.

That is remarkably true, and remarkably sad, and the same remarkably true and sad thing can be said about poetry, here among us today.

SHORT LECTURE ON CRAFT

By 700 BC the Phoenicians were sailing.

We know this because there are records. We know nothing about the time before records.

It is not an easy task, for men to move on water.

So difficult a task is it that as recently as 1940 no one believed that men ignorant of the uses of iron were capable of sailing, let alone navigating, great waters, least of all the greatest of all, the Pacific Ocean; not even professional mariners believed it. But Thor Heyerdahl believed it, he believed that human beings ignorant of the uses of iron, living on what we now call the North and South American Continents, were capable of crossing what we now call the Pacific Ocean, and settling a number of small mountainous islands and flat coral reefs we now call Polynesia.

And so he built a raft, modeled on those the ancient Incans used for fishing in local waters, a raft made from nine Ecuadoran balsa logs lashed together with hemp rope, using no nails, wire, or metal of any kind, a raft with an open bamboo cabin and a crude sail that looked like a piece of cloth hung to dry on a pole, and on this raft, with five companions and a green parrot, he set out, on April 28, 1947, from the coast of Peru, to prove that it was possible.

After 101 days at sea—4,300 miles later—they landed on an uninhabited South Sea island. It had been done. There was now at least one record of such a thing. What was their secret? How did they do it? The secret of the *Kon-Tiki* is that it was a very large cork; their raft rolled with the waves, that's all it could do, it couldn't even turn back. It was cork, and the men who were on it were cork.

A craft is a boat, ship, or airplane; the most primitive craft is a raft, whose very word is embedded in the word *craft*.

Great skill is involved in building a craft, for it is far from easy to make things that float or fly.

Inside the word *raft* is the word *aft*, which means located near the rear, as opposed to the *fore*, which is located near the front.

Fore-and-aft means, therefore, running the length of a craft, from front to rear.

Not top to bottom, front to rear, fore-and-aft.

Before and after: running a length of time, which creates time; without time, there is no length; there is no counting before time.

Before the raft Thor Heyerdahl christened *Kon-Tiki*, after the Incan sun-god, no one thought it possible. But after, men knew that in prehistory, without records, without iron, such a craft existed. Men knew the Phoenicians were not alone. And men knew, too, that it was probable ten such rafts sank to the bottom for every one that sailed.

Those unknown men and women who with the labor of their minds devised a raft and with the labor of their hands tied the logs together and tested the seaworthiness of their raft . . .

Who taught them their craft?

There is of course another meaning of the word *craft*, it is the second or third meaning given in any dictionary.

Craft: skill in evasion or deception.

Those unknown men and women lashing together their gigantic raft, what were they evading, whom were they deceiving? Were they themselves deceived, and evading their deceivers? Were they evading hunger, disaster, unspeakable loss?

We don't know. But surely there must have been a moment of glorious well-being when they slid their raft into the water and discovered that it could float, and would hold them all, as they set out to cut a hole in time.

SHORT LECTURE ON LIVING ALONE

"If I were to be taken beyond the ocean, into Paradise, and forbidden to write, I would refuse the ocean and Paradise." Marina Tsvetayeva.

And what were they anyway, sprigs of grass, things of blue? For a long time I wanted to use words, then didn't.

It is no different than not living alone.

SHORT LECTURE ON POETRY
BY VAN MORRISON

It's quite simple: all you have to do is rave. Rave on. Pass dead bodies over your head; you are, after all, in the pit of life. Rave, raved, raving, raves: to speak wildly, irrationally, or incoherently; to roar, rage. (Please keep in mind the short lecture you have just heard on prayer; sometimes the lowered register accomplishes what the higher register seeks to accomplish.) To speak with wild enthusiasm, to utter in a frenzied manner, to talk wildly as in a delirium of water, wind, storm; to make a wild and furious sound, to rage, to utter as if in madness, like King Lear; an act of appraisal, a review of something such as a play, which, according to Plato and Shakespeare, is a life.

LECTURES I WILL NEVER GIVE

"To live is so startling, it leaves but little room for other occupations."

There are many reasons I don't want to give any of these lectures, and you should probably know it made me angry and sad to have to string together these negations at all.

At the very outset I will tell you that if you think I know something or anything, I am just pretending to know as a way to pass the time. Personally I think we should all be in our rooms writing. Critical components of creative writing are A NECESSARY GESTURE TO VALIDATE THE ENDEAVOR IN THE EYES OF THE ACADEMY WHICH WOULD LIKE OUR BRAINS TO EXPAND. But I like things the size of a pea, I like miniature umbrellas and I like walnuts and I like the part in *Hamlet* where he says he could live in a nutshell and count himself the king of infinite space (were it not for the fact he had bad dreams).

Lectures, for me, are bad dreams.

I'm sometimes reminded of Dawkins's Law of the Conservation of Difficulty, which states that obscurantism in an academic subject expands to fill the vacuum of its intrinsic simplicity.

The problem is compounded by the law of flake-ism, which states that simplicity in an academic subject expands to fill the vacuum of its intrinsic complexity.

I am guilty of both.

In sifting through many, many files in an effort to accumulate debris for this lecture, I came across a few untethered pieces of paper that intrigued me, and I am here to share them with you; they were it seems meant for a lecture, though one I couldn't now write if I tried.

I love pretension. It is a mark of human earthly abstraction, whereas humility is a mark of human divine abstraction. I will

have all of eternity in which to be humble, while I have but a
few short years to be pretentious.

There is a marvelous lecture by Howard Nemerov called
"Speaking Silence," in which he attacks his own profession
(Nemerov was both a poet and a professor). In his address he
urges his audience (teachers) not to confuse "teaching poetry"
with "being taught by poetry."

> Elizabeth dies, bang! comes the first English dictionary.
>   ... about a hundred years [later], ... English first be-
> came a subject of study in college and universities; English
> departments came even after that. . . .
>   Looking at the latter part of this time-lapse film, taking it
> from 1800, say, I submit that what we see, and see, in so
> rapid an overview, overwhelmingly and to the exclusion of
> much else, is an accelerating production of language about
> language, and that this accelerating production also accel-
> erates the rate of its acceleration.

Dr. Johnson could satisfy himself about *Hamlet*, though
not be altogether satisfied with *Hamlet*, in a page and a half.
We cannot do that. Of course, we say, we know more about
Hamlet than Dr. Johnson did. And that is quite true. But,

with a kind of reflexive sadness, what we know is always our own knowledge, never *Hamlet*.

For every use of language about language will tend to produce more language; but the deeper purpose of language is to produce the silence of understanding, the consent between speech and its object, between speaker and hearer . . . that is the end of every great work.

You can imagine my horror when I wanted to give a lecture on this lecture, which would produce nothing but more language on language on language. Even with the tidbits, I've already committed the sacrilege. I'm aware of that. My world, at times, seems choiceless, and it depresses me. Each of us is caught up in a machine that is both of our own making and out of our control. Short of an atom bomb, who among us can escape it? I hope this explains my innate horror of lectures, one of which I am standing here giving.

Kurahashi Yumiko, a Japanese writer born in 1935 who made her debut in the sixties and since then has been largely silent (becoming something of a mystery figure in Japanese letters), wrote this passage in her short story "Ugly Demons," a passage that implicates the reader, too, in being part of the disease, the symptoms of which I so readily recognize in myself:

Although I steeped myself in an incredible amount of reading material, it merely expanded the void, fattened the darkness inside the cactus. Nothing was born from there.... Despite that, I read more and more, growing endlessly fatter of soul until I could not move because of my weight. Just as the mouth takes in food, my eyes avidly devoured everything. No doubt my brain was swelling up from its morbid, chronic hunger. Even after I came to that cottage, my daily task (more even than studying for the university exams) was to continually browse among books like a crazed sheep.

Some primitive tribes have spots of ground reserved as a safe place where they can go and curse the king. Perhaps that is what I am doing here; I am supposing this is a safe spot, and I am cursing the king, whom, when I am living in the village, I secretly loathe and disrespect, and whom, while I am cursing him, I secretly love and am steadfastly devoted to.

Here we are, each of us alive and on earth, all alive and on earth, each of us the envy of every dead man, woman, and child, and—why not?—the envy of each impatient unborn unsexed entity waiting in the great nebula to take its turn on earth. How lucky we are! Yet none of us actually feeling lucky, none of us actually feeling the undeniable fact of the Now. No, each one feeling like a wretched piece of trash not even worth the tossing out, each one feeling envy, greed, boredom, anger, annoyance, conflict, and insecurity. That's the beginning of a lecture called "Quiet Lemons," but I never could find its subject.

"The World's Bleakest Poems." In my research for this lecture I discovered there were too many of them, so I had at that point to change the title of my lecture to "The World's Bleakest Poem." It consisted of a single handout—"To Himself"—by Giacomo Leopardi; here, I will read it to you.

TO HIMSELF

Rest forever, tired heart.
The final illusion has perished.
The one we believed eternal is gone.
Just like that. Out the door desire
follows hope. Rest forever. Enough
throbbing. Nothing deserves your attention
nor is the earth worth a sigh.
Bitterness and boredom is life,
nothing else ever, and mud is the world.

Quiet now. Despair for the last time.
Fate gives us dying as a gift.
Now turn from the hills, the ugly hidden
power there which rules for the common evil
and the infinite vanity of it all.

TRANSLATED BY ARTURO VIVANTE
AND MARY RUEFLE

Right after the big bang, particles of matter and particles of antimatter annihilated each other. But for every billion pairs of particles, there is one extra particle of matter. That tiny imbalance accounts for the existence of poetry, that is, the existence of the observed universe.

A poem is a neutrino—mainly nothing—it has no mass and can pass through the earth undetected.

The lecture in which Lyn Hejinian meets Carl Hiaasen.
The lecture in which Omar Khayyam meets Duran Duran.

Samuel Johnson said, "It is certain that any wild wish or vain imagination never takes such firm possession of the mind, as when it is found empty and unoccupied." He was speaking of melancholy, and how idleness and solitude feed it, undeniably and uncontrollably feed it. We all know this is true, and yet it is equally true that such a state will fund creativity; as artists we understand the vital necessity of wasting time, of loafing and doing nothing, and I was wondering what it is that causes the free and idle mind to go one way or the other—into obsessive melancholy or into creative fervor. What tips the scales, so to speak?

Yeah, that was another subject I let float by.

THE DEER LESSON

One night after dinner at the home of Mark Halliday and Jill Rosser, Mark was driving me back to my place, we were just cruising along chatting idly when suddenly a deer jumped out from nowhere. Mark put on the brakes and shouted, STUPID

DEER, and I simultaneously said, at the same time in the same breath but with an altogether different tone, SWEET DEER, hoping we could get a little closer. Mark said that one of those outbursts leads to writing bad poems, and one of those outbursts leads to writing good poems, and I should call it THE DEER LESSON and walk out of the classroom. But would the students know which outburst Mark had in mind? His, of course; his poem begins with the moment of the encounter and goes on to explain why the human finds the deer stupid and to struggle with their simultaneous existences. My poem is very short and lyrical and basically praises the deer in a sentimental way, my poem speaks in endearing tones to anything that might kill it, and even wishes to come closer to that which might kill it, and in the end both the deer and the driver are simultaneously killed by each other, while in Mark's poem only one or the other dies and the struggle enacted is to determine who dies. In my version, it is apparent and inevitable that both the deer and the driver die together upon contact, thus my poem is shorter and sadder and his is long and thoughtful and the free will of the reader comes into play.

On one piece of paper I had written "the difference between pantyhose and stockings" and I had scanned the statement—

with marks—and written "the beginnings of an iamb," which is
bizarre because I can't scan or recognize an iamb.

And then I began to write a long lecture comparing the two,
their innate and interesting differences, their distinct personal-
ities, their histories and fates; the Second World War played an
important role, and Women's Liberation, not to mention erot-
ica, pornography, technology, poetry, and the imagination. I
came down rather emphatically on the side of stockings, which
was bizarre, as I do not own a single pair of stockings but own
several pairs of pantyhose.

But honestly, do you want me to talk about pantyhose and
stockings for forty minutes?

Natasha Sajé once surveyed a number of women poets and
asked them what influence gender had on their writing and/or
life. I will read to you my answer and you will see from it why
I cannot possibly write a lecture about gender in a way that
matters, for gender is very important in our society and if
people are to speak of it at all they should do so in a way
that matters; when I read the diaries of women I weep, I weep
for women the world over with greater urgency and frequency

as I age, and yet the question of gender in poetry has always bored me.

What influence has your gender had on your writing and/or life?

My gender (female) has had absolutely no influence on my writing; it has had an enormous influence on my life. In my writing I think of myself as a poet, that is, in my writing my gender is poet, while in my life I think of myself as a woman, I have lived my life as a woman, a woman's life. In my writing, gender becomes genre. Of course my life has influenced my writing, that I cannot deny; but I am denying the logic (clearly) that would then link my gender to my writing. I see the logic but I deny it; perhaps this is what makes my gender/genre poetry. In my life, I have a body, that of a woman; in my writing I have only my mind, that of a poet. There is something genderless (sex-wise) about the mind working in the art field; at its best it seems to me, to my mind, to be an encounter between the human mind and the universe, which is without consciousness and without gender. So writing is between mortal self-consciousness and all that it is not, all that is not it. This is true even if I write a poem that is peopled, addressed to persons or to one person, or is "about" something concretely feminine (such as a giving birth)—all these poems are still essentially a mortal self-consciousness exercising its existence, its ability to voice and imagine. The human imagination is a marvelous thing to have evolved on earth, and it did not evolve in one sex of our species only. In the past, it may have been believed that it evolved in one sex of our species only, but that belief was purely cultural (with unfortunate consequences). Even if, as I believe, and believe it has been shown, the minds of men and women have been rigged differently, that is simply circuitry (means) to the same end—mortal self-consciousness, the human imagination. And I am interested in this, the highest end of the wiring. The point of sameness, arrived at by different routes. My proof is that men and women die in the same way, to put it bluntly. The point of sameness in the different bodies. The skeletons retain gender in the width of the hip bones, yes, I don't deny that the difference is still there in the bones, but what of the mind that has vanished? The vanishment is identical—each equally gone. But to return to what I was saying (for I am still alive)—writing is between mortal self-consciousness and all that it is not, all that is not it, while life is carried on between one body and another in a wide variety of relationships and groupings. I never write with another body in the room, changing the flux of my mind. I am absolutely free to do whatever I want, in my writing, until I die, at which point the universe changes my flux of mind by ending it. Diseases of the mind challenge this assumption, but I will not go into that at this time (that would lead us to the question of what constitutes life—health of mind or health of body). In my life I must take into consideration the person with me, and the ways in which a person does that—takes into consideration another person—constitutes one of the great struggles in life, the failures and successes of mutual consideration. Therein lie many tragedies and comedies. In my life I am also bound by cultural and societal restrictions and regulations, some of which I agree to (I do not think I should be free to take off my blouse in a restaurant), some of which I do not agree to (I know with documented certainty I have been paid less than a man for doing identical work). But when I write, I take into consideration not another body but space, abyss, time, pulse, and this encounter constitutes the other great struggle in life—that of the mind in consideration of mindlessness. The simplest I can put it is to say this: my life is the struggle between bodies (mind with minds), while my writing is the struggle between mind and what is without mind. *This is my letter to the World / That never wrote to Me.* I know this line can be interpreted in other ways—ways that take bodies into consideration—but I interpret it as a statement between mind and that which is mindless.

I would like to give a lecture on dolls, but plenty have already done so. In addition, any lecture on dolls winds up being 80 percent Rilke, who has written definitively on the subject. In short, when you were a kid, and you had a soldier or a doll, you invested a real animate life into the inanimate object, and you were experiencing your first act of poetry not when you spoke to them but when they spoke *back to you*, and invested life in *you*, and then this dialogue caused you to believe in the world and the world you could believe in was a world you had created yourself.

New York Times, February 1945:

> DOLLS TOO SAD FOR GOEBBELS. The well known Berlin doll factory of Frau Kate Kruse has been closed by a "special decree" of Propaganda Minister Joseph Goebbels. . . . Frau Kruse, it was said, had given 'sad and desperate faces' to all her dolls since her son was killed in the war.

When a little girl is sad, a doll with a sad face makes her happy.

The problem with many of the poems one sees in workshop is that they differentiate between happiness and sadness. When you do this, your poems have no face.

Once, on the radio, I heard a music announcer say, "We are always suspicious of anything that is not called a masterpiece."

Though I tend to overreact, I almost drove off the road.

My take on it is, we should be suspicious of everything that is called a masterpiece.

One could write a lecture on this.

In a pinch, of course, one can always write about the Dalai Lama . . .

If the Tibetans are as devoted to the idea of impermanence as they say they are, why are they so dedicated to preserving their culture?

Ah, the problem of poetry!

I have been thinking and thinking about this. I have been watching and rewatching a newsreel of His Holiness the Dalai Lama, and listening to him speak. I am charmed and baffled by him. He is so tolerant of everyone he comes in contact with, and yet, he is obviously also, without any attempt to hide it, as inflexible as the hardest metal. I want to use him as the archetype of a sage. Sages are supposed to embody Inner Truth. What is Inner Truth? It is Possession in Great Measure.

Toward men it is accessible, without any pride, without any laying down of the law or desire to assert superior knowledge; within itself, however, it is dignified, free of tormenting doubt, conscious that it stands in the right place.

HELLMUT WILHELM
on hexagram 14 of the *I Ching*

Behind those beneficent crinkly smiles,
behind those mischievous eyes,
behind all that bending and bowing . . .

But it is useless to write about the Dalai Lama because Matthew Zapruder, in his book of poems *The Pajamaist*, has so wonderfully summed it up:

> the Dalai Lama
> is now in Canada, and everyone
> is fascinated. When they come
> to visit me, no one ever leaves me
> saying, the most touching thing
> about him is he's so human.

Spinoza to his former student Albert Burgh:

O brainless youth, who has bewitched you, so that you be-
lieve that you swallow the highest and the eternal, and that
you hold it in your intestines?

A lovely, if somewhat self-serving, lecture could be written
about my experience, three or four years ago, with the Long
Ridge Writers Group, a correspondence course for writers
based in Connecticut. You pay x amount of dollars and work
in the mail one-on-one with an author who will teach you how
to write to publication standards, help you find your writing
niche, and show you how to market your writing. Sound
vaguely familiar? It's a lot like any low-residency program,
without the residencies and the academic sanction of a de-
gree. You have to pass a brief writing test to get in, and one day,
feeling very despondent, and having received their ad-letter
among my junk mail, I decided to take the test and see if I could
be admitted. I wrote very quickly, in longhand, and without
making any changes I mailed the test back. A few weeks later I
got another letter telling me I had passed the aptitude test and
they were ready to enroll me. The interesting thing is that I was
truly elated, and the day the letter came was the best day I had
had in months. I had no money to take the course, and no in-
tention of enrolling, but still. And then when they didn't hear

from me I got another letter telling me that if I enrolled now there would be a price break, and when they still didn't hear from me I got another letter announcing they had chosen my teacher; they included a brochure about her: her name was Anke Kriske, she looked very nice, she has published articles in *Woman's World*, tales in *Alfred Hitchcock's Mystery Magazine*, and a Western whose protagonist was a woman, as well as articles on folklore and history. I really liked her. I felt sorry not to be working with her, I felt guilty, too, and what had started as a lark became a dark secret, and I felt that by not enrolling I was truly passing up what might be my last chance to become a better writer. Letters like these kept coming, and then they stopped, and when they stopped I missed them. The problem with this lecture is that it would sound like a hoax, and people would laugh, and I knew I could neither convey nor convince people to believe the real emotional turmoil the letters caused me. I saved every one of them, and I still have them, and take them out and look at them from time to time.

I've always wanted to give a lecture on literary manifestos, since I happen to have a copy of every manifesto ever publicly disseminated. But why bother? My conclusion to that lecture is: manifestos, although they can be a lot of fun, rapidly become dated and are basically a crock of shit.

For years I wanted to write a lecture titled "The Impossibility of Romanticism Developing above the Arctic Circle." At the same time I always felt that its premise was completely obvious: Romanticism developed in a temperate climate, one with four distinct seasons, because the cycles of the Romantic imagination mirror the natural cycles of such an environment, and the greatest Romantic poets fall within a circle that can be mapped on the globe, and it's an obvious fact that the English and German and French Romantic poets were greater than, say, the great Greek and Moroccan Romantic poets. I just had the feeling that I would be perceived as a dodo bird.

Now the dodo bird is another interesting topic, and one of particular interest to me because when I was a child my brother and sister would call me a dodo bird and then go get the encyclopedia and show me pictures of the dodo bird, which was clumsy, fat, dumb, and big-headed—and it couldn't fly. Dodo birds flourished on the island of Mauritius in the Indian Ocean until humans arrived and began to eat them, and their babies, and their eggs. The humans introduced pigs and monkeys to the island, who began to eat the dodoes, and their babies, and their eggs. The poor flightless dodoes hadn't a chance, and were extinct by 1690. I believe that all poets are winged, and some can fly and some cannot, and that having wings is their distinguishing feature, not whether they can fly. Some poets can fly but they don't have wings and they are the worse. If you are trying to fly, stop it. Just watch under your arms for signs of wings, and if they sprout, even if you can't ever make it off the ground, say you are a turkey—well, that is an interesting thing. Of course you may be a lark, and that would be lucky. But in general pay attention to the wings, not to the sky.

Very recently I was talking to a poet who has, like me, a keen interest in life above the Arctic Circle, and she helped me to understand that poetry coming from the Arctic Circle is much more of our times than Romanticism. It came about like this: I asked her if she was happier reading *Kabloona* (a classic tale by a white man living among the Inuit, circa 1930) or one of her books on capitalism (for she is also a Marxist); she had been blue, you see, and I wanted her to be happier, I wanted her to read more books like *Kabloona* and fewer tomes on capitalism; and she said, astonishingly: Oh, the capitalism. I asked her to explain. She said that *Kabloona* was like an introductory book on capitalism but a book on capitalism was the real thing, an expanded version of *Kabloona*, because capitalism, like the Arctic environment, is a system THAT DOESN'T CARE IF YOU LIVE OR DIE—capitalism is *worldwide* Arctic conditions, and we are living in them and thus it was even more chilling!

Here is a poem by Rilke:

[EXPOSED ON THE CLIFFS OF THE HEART]

Exposed on the cliffs of the heart. Look, how tiny down
   there,
look: the last village of words and, higher,
(but how tiny) still one last
farmhouse of feeling. Can you see it?
Exposed on the cliffs of the heart. Stoneground
under your hands. Even here, though,
something can bloom; on a silent cliff-edge
an unknowing plant blooms, singing, into the air.
But the one who knows? Ah, he began to know
and is quiet now, exposed on the cliffs of the heart.
While, with their full awareness,
many sure-footed mountain animals pass
or linger. And the great sheltered bird flies, slowly
circling, around the peak's pure denial.—But
without a shelter, here on the cliffs of the heart. . . .

And Samuel Beckett, in an interview: "I speak of an art turn-
ing from [the plane of the feasible] in disgust, weary of puny
exploits, weary of pretending to be able, of being able, of do-
ing a little better the same old thing, of going a little further
along a dreary road."

And preferring what? the interviewer asked.

"The expression that there is nothing to express, nothing with which to express, nothing from which to express, no power to express, no desire to express, together with the obligation to express."

This has got to stop. Can you see what I am doing? I am beginning to write a lecture.

The lecture in which I talk about every single word in a given poem, devoting the most amount of time to the first word (and I would choose a poem in which the first word was either *A* or *The*,) and a proportionately diminishing amount of time on each subsequent word, reserving the least amount of time for the last word.

Lecture on this astounding object, a candle in the shape of an ice-cream cone, which represents to me a poem. At first glance it is merely cute, at second glance merely witty, but at third glance demonstrates the profound capacity of metaphor to link two unlike things, and at fourth glance leads us to the astonishing realization that these two things were *all along* obviously alike and, finally, so overwhelming as to reconstitute the ghost of Rimbaud, so thoroughly does this object disorder our senses: a candle in the shape of an ice-cream cone. One may be hot and one may be cold, but the object of both is to disappear, and to drip while doing so.

I like best the idea of writing a lecture on a photograph. One photograph I adore, and keep always by me, shows Samuel Beckett, Alberto Giacometti, and a young critic/admirer whose name I do not know standing in a gallery where Giacometti's set for *Waiting for Godot* is on display (though you can't see it)—a single tree. If you know Giacometti's work, you can imagine it. The photo was taken in the early sixties, before Giacometti died, and in it Beckett and Giacometti are looking up, up, up at the tree: Beckett has the look of someone praying before a crucifix, and Giacometti has a slightly more self-conscious look, as if admiring the thing but also hoping someone else might see in it what he sees in it—which is only natural, as he himself made the thing; and the young critic/admirer is not looking at the thing at all, he is looking at Beckett and Giacometti. He is much, much younger than they are, and he does not see the Thing; he sees the two men instead, because it is obvious he mistakes them for the Thing, and he is not there to see the Thing, he is there to see what he takes for the Thing, the two men. While the two men are looking at the Thing.

There is another picture I would like to write about, and as perhaps one day I will, it is perhaps unfair to mention it. It is a photograph of Robert Walser taken by the coroner on the day of his death, December 25, 1956. When the children discovered Walser's body lying on its back in the snow, the coroner was called and he came and a series of photographs were taken. As it happened, I first saw the photographs on Christmas Day, fifty years after they were taken. The most chilling thing is not Walser himself but the footprints in the snow leading up to the body, Walser's footprints as he was walking and then fell, as he was walking toward his death and met it there, and I cannot look at the photograph without noticing the faint wooden stakes in the background, a snowed-upon fence he was about to meet, and then I remember Kafka, who wrote once that he was a slanting wooden stake in a snowfield at dusk, and it was snowing.

Once I wanted to write a lecture on two self-portraits by the German artist Käthe Kollwitz, who lived in the late nineteenth and early twentieth centuries and achieved recognition when it was still extremely rare for women artists.

Single self-portraits are not half as interesting as two self-portraits by the same artist painted thirty or forty years apart. When Käthe painted herself as a young woman she had a very pale and serene face against a dark background. Her hand rested on an open book. She was reading by lamplight. She was, obviously, a young woman with an inner life, and the portrait is composed as if to say, "I am a sensitive, curious, intelligent being, and in my search for knowledge and experience I will learn all there is to know about the world around me—here, I give you my pledge by placing my hand on this *open book*." It is a nineteenth-century oil painting of quiet and penetrating elegance.

Thirty-five years later she draws herself again—for it's a drawing this time and not a painting—with excruciating rapidity. Her face is scrawled in black ink out of a series of highly agitated circles and at a distance might easily be mistaken for a tightly wound clockspring. Gone is the book—this time her hand appears to be driving itself into her forehead with the force of a nail. She's pressing her head so hard the viewer is taken aback.

This twentieth-century drawing says, "All that was to be known was *inside* me and bit by bit it did its work and made this tormented and exhausted head." Her face has *become* the open book.

But that's a lecture that has to be lived.

The composer Dmitry Shostakovich's certainty that musical notes radiated from a piece of shrapnel lodged in his brain.

I have always believed I became a writer because in the fifth grade I had a pencil fight with a classmate and a piece of graphite has been lodged in my palm ever since.

If art were about intellect there would be no artists there would be only intellectuals.

Someone gave me a lecture this summer. A woman I know very, very, very slightly was sitting next to me at a lake where we had come to swim. As it happens, the lake has been the backdrop of my life, and I was looking out at a raft that was so rotted and bleached and lopsided that it was apparent its life was nearly finished. This made me sad, for I loved that raft; in fact, if you were to look inside my wallet right now, as it sleeps quietly in my purse, you would find a picture of the raft tucked in a secret compartment.

In a rare moment of emotional candor I turned to this woman and told her how sad I was sitting there looking at the dilapi-

dated raft. That was when she gave me her lecture. "YOU'RE
SO NEGATIVE! STOP IDENTIFYING WITH A PIECE OF
WOOD! IT'S NOT YOU! SNAP OUT OF IT!"

I went into something resembling shock. That is not a lecture
I could give—it's not something I believe in. The next day I re-
turned to the lake and the raft was gone.

> Bin of animals
> at the Goodwill—
> all my friends
> in one place.

For a long, long time I wanted to write a lecture called "Asy-
lum." An asylum is a secure place of refuge, shelter, or retreat.
It is a sanctuary, an inviolable place from which one cannot be
removed without sacrilege. An asylum is a benevolent institu-
tion affording shelter and protection to some class of the af-
flicted. It is also an insane place, full of shouts and cries and
cries and whispers. An asylum is a place of hopeless suffering
and endless misunderstanding, a place of restriction and des-
peration. I like the word *asylum*. Poetry is an asylum to me. Do
you know what insanity is? Insanity is "doing the same thing
over and over, expecting different results." That's writing po-

etry, but hey, it's also getting out of bed every morning. The argument over madness can be reduced to this: madness is excluded from thought vs. madness is "one *case* of thought (*within* thought)" (Derrida). The whole history of poetry could ensue from such a discussion. I don't want to have it.

Once I spent hours in a room trying to decide which was more accurate:

I am paved with purple rushes

or

I am paid with purple thrushes

I was in agony, trying to decide.

According to the research of Arnold Ludwig, among all persons of all professions mental disorders appear most among artists. Among all artists, mental disorders appear most among writers. Among all writers, mental disorders appear most among poets.

I am perfectly capable of writing a thirty-page essay titled "Asylum." In fact, I have made hundreds of notes over the last five years in that direction, and I am going to pass them all out, among you, today. I don't want them. You can have them. The lecture on asylums I want to give has already been given. It was given on November 18, 2000, in Northampton, Massachusetts, by the extraordinary installation artist Anna Schuleit. The Northampton State Hospital, a gothic monstrosity the size of a castle and sitting on a hill, was in continuous operation from 1856 to 1993. Its history is no different than the history of similar institutions all over this country, institutions I researched for years and planned to speak about, in detail, in my lecture called "Asylum."

In the year 2000 the Northampton State Hospital was slated for demolition. It was in a state of complete physical collapse, with broken windows, missing walls, and flooded interiors. It was therefore no mean thing for Anna to wire the entire building and on that glorious autumn day to blast, for 25 minutes and 46 seconds, J. S. Bach's great choral work, the *Magnificat*, from every window, door, and portal that still remained.

For 25 minutes and 46 seconds the building sang. It sang "*for those who have been there*," all the men, women, and children who ever lived within its walls; men, women, and children for whom the asylum was a place of refuge; men, women, and children for whom the asylum was a place of torment and final shattering. Some of them were still living and stood on the grounds. What are words next to that?

Now I will give you a piece of advice. I will tell you something that I absolutely believe you should do, and if you do not do it you will never be a writer. It is a certain truth.

When your pencil is dull, sharpen it.

And when your pencil is sharp, use it until it is dull again.

For me, there is no difference between writing and drawing. Both are uncanny miracles that result from the act of taking one thing—an implement, a tool—and touching it to another thing —anything that will serve as a surface—and beholding a third thing born of that contact: a mark. If you don't believe me, take a pencil and put it on a piece of paper, move it using your hand, exerting a little downward pressure—you might even want to let your hand tremble with emotion at the prospect of being engaged in such a miracle—and see what is created there: a mark.

But when I watch people drawing and people writing I notice a difference: when people draw they constantly look up at the thing they are drawing, and when people write their eyes never leave the page. Why is this, I wonder, and what is going on? At first I thought the drawer was drawing what he sees, externally, while the writer was drawing what he sees internally, that which

is in his mind. But when I thought longer and harder I remem-
bered that some people indeed draw without looking at any-
thing and therefore never look up. What is going on, I thought:
What are these people doing and will I ever know? I wish I
could talk to paper. I want to know if the paper is happy or sad
when someone makes a mark on it. But if I knew that it was sad,
being so marked upon, would I stop marking? Probably not,
and thus all creative activity stems from a violent impulse—the
willed impulse to interfere, to interrupt, to mar, to stop. I sup-
pose it is sad, but this kind of violent activity makes me happy.
When I make contact with a piece of paper without looking up
I am happy. I call this writing a poem. It is a moment of draw-
ing happiness. I am drawing a picture of happiness.

Now my lecture has ended, and I am free, and happy, as I was
meant to be.

Then we fell to talking of the burning of the City;
and Lady Carteret herself did tell us how abundance
of pieces of burnt papers were cast by the wind as far as
Cranborne; and among others she took up one, or had
one brought her to see, which was a little bit of paper
that had been printed, whereon there remained no
more nor less than these words: "Time is, it is done."

SAMUEL PEPYS

ACKNOWLEDGMENTS

"On Beginnings" appeared in the anthology *Words Overflown by Stars* (Story Press, 2009). "Poetry and the Moon" appeared in the anthology *Open Book: Essays from the Vermont College Postgraduate Writers' Conference* (Cambridge Scholars Publishing, 2006). "On Sentimentality" and "On Theme" were previously published in *West Branch*. "On Secrets" was previously published in *Third Coast*. "Someone Reading a Book Is a Sign of Order in the World" was written for the anthology *Planet on the Table: Poets on the Reading Life* (Sarabande Books, 2003), yet the present essay has been extended by the addition of several sections. "Kangaroo Beach" appeared in *American Poet*, the journal of the Academy of American Poets. "Twenty-Two Short Lectures" was published in *Bat City Review*. "Lectures I Will Never Give" appeared in *Eleven Eleven*.

"I Remember, I Remember" owes its form, of course, to the wonderful Joe Brainard.

SELECTED BIBLIOGRAPHY

I always read with a pencil in my hand—according to George Steiner, this makes me an intellectual! But how can I be, when I never, in all my word-taking, write the name of the book I am taking words from—I write only the words, and their author. The following list is the result of the Herculean effort of the Wave Books staff, and to them I bow; and if any reader finds a missing or erroneous source, let him contemplate in quietude how best to spend his days.

Akhmatova, Anna. *Complete Poems of Anna Akhmatova.* Trans. Judith Hemschemeyer. Cambridge, MA: Zephyr Press, 1992.

Alighieri, Dante. *Purgatorio.* Trans. W. S. Merwin. New York: Alfred A. Knopf, 2000.

Ashbery, John. *Flow Chart.* New York: Alfred A. Knopf, 1991.

Auden, W. H. *Collected Poems.* Ed. Edward Mendelson. New York: Random House, 1976.

Auster, Paul. *Moon Palace.* New York: Penguin Books, 1989.

Bachelard, Gaston. *The Poetics of Space.* Trans. Maria Jolas. Boston: Beacon Press, 1994 ed.

———. *Water and Dreams.* Trans. Edith R. Farrell. Dallas: Pegasus Foundation, 1983.

Barthes, Roland. *The Eiffel Tower and Other Mythologies*. Trans. Richard Howard. Berkeley: University of California Press, 1997.

———. *Roland Barthes*. Trans. Richard Howard. New York: Hill and Wang, 1977.

Bataille, Georges. *The Tears of Eros*. Trans. Peter Connor. San Francisco: City Lights Books, 1989.

Beckett, Samuel. *The Grove Centenary Edition*. Ed. Paul Auster. New York: Grove Press, 2006.

Berg, Stephen. *In Praise of What Persists* (editor). New York: Harper and Row, 1983.

Berger, John. *Photocopies*. New York: Pantheon Books, 1996.

Bergson, Henri. *An Introduction to Metaphysics*. Trans. T. E. Hulme. New York: Liberal Arts Press, 1949.

Bernard, Mary. *Sappho: A New Translation*. Berkeley: University of California Press, 1999.

Berryman, John. *The Dream Songs*. New York: Farrar, Straus and Giroux, 1969.

Blanchot, Maurice. Afterword (Trans. Lydia Davis) for *Notebooks of Joseph Joubert*. Ed. Paul Auster. San Francisco: North Point Press, 1983.

Bly, Robert. *Neruda and Vallejo: Selected Poems*. New York: Beacon Press, 1993.

Bogan, Louise. *A Poet's Prose: Selected Writings of Louise Bogan*. Ed. Mary Kinzie. Athens, OH: Swallow Press / Ohio University Press, 2005.

Bonnefoy, Yves. *In the Shadow's Light*. Trans. John Naughton. Chicago: University of Chicago Press, 1991.

Borges, Jorge Luis. *Atlas* (with María Kodama). Trans. Anthony Kerrigan. New York: Dutton, 1985.

Bronk, William. *Manifest and Furthermore*. San Francisco: North Point Press, 1987.

Brontë, Emily. *Poems*. London: Fount, 1996.

Cage, John. *A Year from Monday: New Lectures and Writing*. Middletown, CT: Wesleyan, 1967.

Carruth, Hayden. *Tell Me Again How the White Heron Rises and Flies Across the Nacreous River at Twilight Toward the Distant Islands*. New York: New Directions, 1989.

Clare, John. *John Clare: Selected Letters*. Ed. Mark Storey. Oxford: Clarendon Press, 1988.

———. *Selected Poems of John Clare*. Ed. Geoffrey Grigson. Cambridge, MA: Harvard University Press, 1950.

Coleridge, Samuel Taylor. *The Notebooks of Samuel Taylor Coleridge*, vol. 1, *1794–1804*. Ed. Kathleen Coburn. Bollingen Series L. New York: Pantheon Books, 1957.

Colette. *Earthly Paradise*. New York: Farrar, Straus and Giroux, 1966.

Collins, Billy. *Picnic, Lightning*. Pittsburgh: University of Pittsburgh Press, 1998.

Crane, Hart. *Complete Poems of Hart Crane*. Ed. Marc Simon. New York: Liveright, 1993.

———. *The Letters of Hart Crane, 1916–1932*. Ed. Brom Weber. New York: Hermitage House, 1952.

Darwin, Charles. *The Life and Letters of Charles Darwin*. Ed. Francis Darwin. New York: Basic Books, 1959.

Derrida, Jacques. *Writing and Difference*. Trans. Alan Bass. Chicago: University of Chicago Press, 1978.

Dickinson, Emily. *The Letters of Emily Dickinson*. Ed. Thomas H. Johnson. Cambridge, MA: The Belknap Press of Harvard University Press, 1958.

———. *The Master Letters of Emily Dickinson*. Ed. R. W. Franklin. Amherst: Amherst College Press, 1986.

———. *The Poems of Emily Dickinson*. Ed. Thomas H. Johnson. Cambridge, MA: The Belknap Press of Harvard University Press, 1955.

Dinesen, Isak. *Out of Africa*. New York: Random House, 1938.

Dunlop, Lane. *Autumn Wind and Other Stories* (translator). Rutland, VT: Charles E. Tuttle, 1994.

Emerson, Ralph Waldo. *The Essential Writings of Ralph Waldo Emerson*. Ed. Brooks Atkinson. New York: The Modern Library, 2000.

Fenton, James. *An Introduction to English Poetry*. New York: Macmillan, 2004.

Fitzgerald, Penelope. *The Blue Flower*. London: Flamingo, 1995.

Frank, Anne. *Diary of a Young Girl: The Definitive Edition*. Ed. Otto H. Frank and Mirjam Pressler. Trans. Susan Massotty. New York: Doubleday, 1995.

Frost, Robert. *Notebooks of Robert Frost*. Ed. Robert Faggen. Cambridge, MA: The Belknap Press of Harvard University Press, 2006.

Gide, André. *The White Notebook*. Trans. Wade Baskin. London: Peter Owen, 1967.

Glück, Louise. *Proofs and Theories: Essays on Poetry*. Hopewell, NJ: Ecco, 1994.

Gombrowicz, Witold. *Diary*, vol. 1. Trans. Lillian Vallee. Evanston, IL: Northwestern University Press, 1988.

Grahame, Kenneth. *The Wind in the Willows*. New York: Viking Press, 1983.

Hall, Donald. *Their Ancient Glittering Eyes: Remembering Poets and More Poets*. Boston: Ticknor and Fields, 1992.

Heckscher, August. *The Public Happiness*. New York: Atheneum, 1962.

Herbert, Zbigniew. *The Collected Prose: 1948–1998*. Ed. Alissa Valles. New York: Ecco, 2010.

Høeg, Peter. *Smilla's Sense of Snow*. Trans. Tiina Nunnally. New York: Farrar, Straus and Giroux, 1993.

Hopkins, Gerard Manley. *The Poems of Gerard Manley Hopkins*, 4th ed. Ed. W. H. Gardner and N. H. MacKenzie. London: Oxford University Press, 1967.

Ibuse, Masuji. *Black Rain: A Novel*. Trans. John Bester. New York: Kodansha USA, 1988.

Jabès, Edmond. *The Book of Questions*. Trans. Rosmarie Waldrop. Middletown, CT: Wesleyan University Press, 1976-1977.

Julian of Norwich. *Revelations of Divine Love*. Ed./Trans. Clifton Wolters. Baltimore: Penguin Books, 1966.

Jung, Carl Gustav. *Collected Works of C. G. Jung*. Ed. Herbert Read, Michael Scott Fordham, and Gerhard Adler. New York: Princeton University Press, 1970.

Kafka, Franz. *Dearest Father: Stories and Other Writings*. Trans.

Ernst Kaiser and Eithne Wilkins. New York: Schocken Books, 1954.

——. *The Diaries of Franz Kafka: 1914–1923.* Ed. Max Brod. Trans. Martin Greenberg with the cooperation of Hannah Arendt. New York: Schocken Books, 1949.

——. *The Penguin Complete Short Stories of Franz Kafka.* Ed. Nahum N. Glatzer. London: Allen Lane, 1983.

Keats, John. *Selected Poems and Letters.* Ed. Douglas Bush. Boston: Houghton Mifflin, 1959.

——. *The Poems of John Keats.* Ed. Jack Stillinger. Cambridge, MA: The Belknap Press of Harvard University Press, 1978.

Kierkegaard, Søren. *A Kierkegaard Anthology.* Ed. Robert Bretall. Princeton: Princeton University Press, 1947.

Lamb, Charles. *The Complete Works and Letters of Charles Lamb* (The Modern Library). New York: Random House, 1935.

Larkin, Philip. *The Less Deceived.* Hessle, East Yorkshire: The Marvell Press, 1955.

Lévi-Strauss, Claude. *Tristes Tropiques.* Trans. John and Doreen Weightman. New York: Penguin, 1992.

Lindwer, Willy. *The Last Seven Months of Anne Frank.* Trans. Alison Meersschaert. New York: Pantheon Books, 1991.

Lispector, Clarice. *Selected Crônicas.* Trans. Giovanni Pontiero. New York: New Directions, 1992.

Livon-Grosman, Ernesto. *José Lezama Lima: Selections* (editor). Berkeley: University of California Press, 2005.

Lopez, Barry. *Arctic Dreams.* New York: Charles Scribner's Sons, 1986.

Lowell, Robert. *Collected Poems*. Ed. Frank Bidart and David Gewanter. New York: Farrar, Straus and Giroux, 2003.

MacLeish, Archibald. *Collected Poems, 1917–1952*. New York: Houghton Mifflin, 1952.

Mann, Thomas. *Death in Venice*. Trans. Kenneth Burke. New York: Alfred A. Knopf, 1965.

Melville, Herman. *Pierre; or, The Ambiguities*. Evanston: Northwestern University Press; Chicago: The Newberry Library, 1971.

Merton, Thomas. *The Other Side of the Mountain: The End of the Journey*. San Francisco: HarperSanFrancisco, 1998.

Miłosz , Czesław. *The Witness of Poetry*. Cambridge, MA: Harvard University Press, 1983.

Montale, Eugenio. *It Depends: A Poet's Notebook*. Trans. G. Singh. New York: New Directions, 1980.

Nabokov, Vladimir. *The Stories of Vladimir Nabokov*. Trans. Vladimir Nabokov and Dmitri Nabokov. New York: Vintage Books, 1997.

Negroponte, Nicholas. *Being Digital*. New York: Alfred A. Knopf, 1995.

Nemerov, Howard. *Figures of Thought: Speculations on the Meaning of Poetry and Other Essays*. Boston: David R. Godine, 1978.

Neruda, Pablo. *Passions and Impressions*. Ed. Matilde Neruda and Miguel Otero Silva. Trans. Margaret Sayers Peden. New York: Farrar, Straus and Giroux, 1983.

———. *Residence on Earth*. Trans. Donald D. Walsh. New York: New Directions, 1973.

Nhat Hanh, Thich. *Cultivating the Mind of Love*. Berkeley, CA: Parallax Press, 2008.

Nietzsche, Friedrich Wilhelm. *Thus Spoke Zarathustra: A Book for All and None*. Trans. Walter Kaufmann. New York: Viking Penguin, 1966.

Pawel, Ernst. *The Nightmare of Reason: A Life of Franz Kafka*. New York: Farrar, Straus and Giroux, 1984.

Pepys, Samuel. *The Diary of Samuel Pepys*. Ed. Robert Latham and William Matthews. London: HarperCollins, 1995.

Queneau, Raymond. *Letters, Numbers, Forms: Essays, 1928–70*. Trans. Jordan Stump. Urbana: University of Illinois Press, 2007.

Ransom, John Crowe. *The World's Body*. New York: Charles Scribner's Sons, 1938.

Rilke, Rainer Maria. *The Notebooks of Malte Laurids Brigge*. Trans. M. D. Herter Norton. New York: W.W. Norton, 1964.

———. *The Selected Poetry of Rainer Maria Rilke*. Edited and Trans. Stephen Mitchell. New York: Random House, 1982.

Roethke, Theodore. *The Collected Poems of Theodore Roethke*. New York: Doubleday, 1966.

Salter, James. *Burning the Days*. New York: Random House, 1998.

Sebald, W. G. *The Rings of Saturn*. Trans. Michael Hulse. New York: New Directions, 1998.

Seferis, George. "A Poet's Journal." In *The Poet's Work: 29 Masters of 20th Century Poetry on the Origins and Practice of Their Art*. Ed. Reginald Gibbons. Boston: Houghton Mifflin, 1979.

Shelley, Mary. *Frankenstein*. Ed. Johanna M. Smith. Boston: Bedford/St. Martin's, 2000.

Shelley, Percy Bysshe. *The Major Works*. Ed. Zachary Leader and Michael O'Neill. Oxford: Oxford University Press, 2003.

Shorter, Clement King. *Charlotte Brontë and Her Circle*. New York: Dodd, Mead and Company, 1896.

Simic, Charles. *The Monster Loves His Labyrinth: Notebooks*. Keene, NY: Ausable Press, 2008.

———. *The Unemployed Fortune-Teller: Essays and Memoirs*. Ann Arbor: University of Michigan Press, 1994.

Smith, Barbara Herrnstein. *Poetic Closure: A Study of How Poems End*. Chicago: University of Chicago Press, 1968.

Spark, Muriel and Derek Stanford. *Emily Brontë: Her Life and Work*. New York: Coward-McCann, 1966.

Spinoza. *The Correspondence of Spinoza*. Translated and Ed. A. Wolf. New York: The Dial Press, 1966.

Stein, Gertrude. *Everybody's Autobiography*. Cambridge, MA: Exact Change, 1993.

Stevens, Wallace. *The Collected Poems of Wallace Stevens*. New York: Alfred A. Knopf, 1954.

———. *The Letters of Wallace Stevens*. Selected and Ed. Holly Stevens. Berkeley: University of California Press, 1996.

Tranströmer, Tomas. *Selected Poems, 1954–1986*. Ed. Robert Hass. New York: Ecco, 1987.

Tsvetayeva, Marina. *Selected Poems*. Trans. Elaine Feinstein. London: Oxford University Press, 1971.

Valéry, Paul. *Collected Works of Paul Valery*, vol. 13, *Aesthetics*. Trans. Ralph Manheim. Princeton: Princeton University Press, 1956.

Venturi, Robert, Denise Scott Brown, and Steven Izenour. *Learning from Las Vegas*. Cambridge, MA: The MIT Press, 1972.

Vicuña, Cecilia. *Unravelling Words and the Weaving of Water*. Trans. Eliot Weinberger and Suzanne Jill Levine. Saint Paul, MN: Graywolf Press, 1992.

Whitman, Walt. *Leaves of Grass*. Ed. Jerome Loving. Oxford: Oxford University Press, 1990.

———. *Leaves of Grass: The First (1855) Edition*. 150th anniversary edition. New York: Penguin, 2005.

Wilhelm, Hellmut. *Heaven, Earth, and Man in The Book of Changes: Seven Eranos Lectures*. Seattle: University of Washington Press, 1977.

Wittgenstein, Ludwig. *Zettel*. Trans. G.E.M. Anscombe. Berkeley: University of California Press, 1967.

Wordsworth, William. *The Major Works*. Ed. Stephen Gill. Oxford: Oxford University Press.

Yeats, W. B. *The Collected Works of W.B. Yeats*, vol. 1, *The Poems*. Ed. Richard J. Finneran. New York: Macmillan, 1989.

———. *A Vision: A Reissue with the Author's Final Revisions*. New York: Collier Books, 1956.

Zagajewski, Adam. *Polish Writers on Writing*. San Antonio, TX: Trinity University Press, 2007.

Zapruder, Matthew. *The Pajamaist*. Port Townsend, WA: Copper Canyon Press, 2006.

PERMISSIONS

K felt he
was a
slanting
wooden
stake
in a snow
field at
dusk

ML 12/13